Moe   Larry   Curly

To Lee

RUBBER
BALLS
AND LIQUOR

RUBBER BALLS AND LIQUOR

GILBERT GOTTFRIED

ST. MARTIN'S PRESS
NEW YORK

RUBBER BALLS AND LIQUOR. Copyright © 2011 by Gilbert Gottfried.
All rights reserved. Printed in the United States of America.
For information, address St. Martin's Press, 175 Fifth Avenue,
New York, N.Y. 10010.

www.stmartins.com

Library of Congress Cataloging-in-Publication Data

Gottfried, Gilbert, 1955–
    Rubber balls and liquor / Gilbert Gottfried. — 1st ed.
        p. cm.
    ISBN 978-0-312-66811-2
    1. Gottfried, Gilbert, 1955–   2. Comedians—United States—Biography.
3. Actors—United States—Biography.   4. American wit and humor.   I. Title.
    PN2287.G656A3 2011
    792.7'6028092—dc22

                                                            2010054558

First Edition: May 2011

10   9   8   7   6   5   4   3   2   1

To Lillian and Lily and both Maxes

CONTENTS

This is the page where brilliant writers like myself look to other brilliant writers for a few words of inspiration to start their book. I've looked and looked, but haven't been able to find anything as brilliant as I could come up with on my own, so I figured I would just write this part myself. Plus, someone at the publishing house mentioned I might have to pay a fee or get permission to use a quote from someone else, and I was like, Yeah, right.

—GILBERT GOTTFRIED

RUBBER BALLS AND LIQUOR

INTRODUCTION

A Slice of Pizza and a Grape Drink

If I knew one day I'd write a book, I would have tried to live a more interesting life. I would have discovered fire, or invented the wheel, or added more fiber to my diet. Absolutely, I would have done . . . something. But then again, it's just as well, because if I know me (and I like to think I do), I would have kept all that good stuff to myself. I mean, it's nobody's business who I slept with, who I cheated in business, who I snubbed at a Friars Club roast. It's not even anybody's business *whom* I slept with or cheated or snubbed, or whether I prefer the subjective or objective pronoun. That's between me and my editor.

Most people, when I tell them I'm writing a book, they have two reactions. Either they look at me like I'm kidding, or like I'm full of shit. They'll say, "Gilbert, why are you writing a book? Do you have anything to say?" And I'll say, "No, not really."

In my experience that's not why most people write books—because they have something to say. It's not like I read newspapers or watch the news, so I certainly don't have anything topical to say about current events or trends. Who has time for that sort of thing? By the time I hear about some new development, it's usually old news and something else has already happened. Plus, you never know what to believe. Just the other day, I heard that a black man had been elected President of the United States, and I had to laugh. I mean, where do they get some of this shit? Next they'll be telling me that a *blind* black man is, say, the governor of New York, or that Angelina Jolie is a revered social icon and humanitarian who no longer wears the blood of her lovers in a vial draped around her neck.

And so, if I have nothing to say, what the hell am I doing writing a book? It's a perfectly reasonable question. And, it just so happens that I've got a perfectly reasonable answer: I'm writing a book because I have a book deal.

Think of it in movie terms. I was once at a party and overheard these Hollywood types discussing Tom Cruise. One guy said Tom Cruise owed the studio one more picture. Another guy said he had three top directors ready to sign on to the project and a major distribution deal here and abroad. A third guy said, "Great, so what should the movie be about?"

Well, it's the same with books. Some guy set up a book deal for me, so now I have to write it. Nobody ever said, "Boy, Gilbert Gottfried is a fascinating intellect. He should write a book." Now, I'm fairly certain that a great many people have thought this very thing, over the years, but I don't believe anyone has dared to speak such a thought out loud. As far as I know, there are no "What Would Gilbert Do?" bumper stickers out there in the heartland, indicating a burning or possibly even chafing desire on the part of Middle Americans to know what Gilbert Gottfried might say or think or do, in a given situation. But now that there's this book deal in place, I might as well follow through on it and tell them anyway. Who knows, maybe I'll come up with something memorable. Maybe I'll come off sounding like one of the great comic minds of my generation. Wouldn't that be a kick in the ass?

You may have noticed that this isn't one of those "as told to" books. Maybe you didn't notice it at first, because I slipped so naturally into a writing style that seemed to match my charming onstage personality. It must have left some readers thinking, *There's no way Gilbert could have written these few sentences by himself.* Ah, but that's where you're wrong, dear reader. I sharpened a couple pencils and sat down at my desk and wrote these few sentences, and then a few more besides. (This sentence right here, inside these parentheses, I'm writing *right now*—as we speak, so to speak.) Yes, it would have been so much easier to hire a professional writer to do it all for me, but there's no fooling you, is there? You're too smart for that.

Oh, wait. Scratch that. If you were *really* smart, you wouldn't be reading this book.

Me, I'm just smart enough to know that I'm an irritatingly voiced comic who hasn't written a good dick joke since the Carter administration. Basically, I've been getting by all these years on my charm and good looks and winsome personality.

(*Winsome*, lose some . . . take your pick.)

If you're like me, you've probably always hated "as told to" books. You read them and think, *Okay, is this the famous guy talking, or is this the "as told to" guy talking?* Or, *Is this what the famous guy really means to say, or have his words been twisted and neutered and sucked clean of human emotion and genuine feeling?* It's too confusing.

Say what you will about Adolf Hitler. (Go ahead, say it.) When he sat down to write *Mein Kampf,* he sat down to write *Mein Kampf.* Check out the cover and see if I'm right. It doesn't say *Mein Kampf,* by Adolf Hitler, as told to Murray Kaplowitz. It's just *der Führer,* putting it all on the line, doing his own thing. I read that and think, *Good for you, Adolf,* because now I know how hard it is to write one of these things. Turns out they want you to say something interesting on every damn page.

If you've seen my act, you'll know that I say whatever pops into my head, very often without a conscious thought. This can be a problem in the literary field, I'm told, where it sometimes helps to think things through. Also, you'll know if you've seen my act that I'm not the sort of person who writes things down—which I'm now learning is counterproductive when it comes to writing a book, where writing things down can actually be helpful.

(If you *haven't* seen my act, then you've got no business reading these opening remarks. Surely, there's a more appropriate book you could have chosen on which to waste your time and hard-earned money. Do you mean to tell me that in this entire bookstore, with rows and rows of shelves and hundreds and hundreds of different titles, you couldn't find another book to capture your attention? There are tons of other books in the store that might be a better choice. Perhaps you should try the Gardening section. Or, Bird Watching. Or, if you're determined to read the musings of a short, whiny Jew, you might consider something by Morey Amsterdam.)

So here's my idea: I'll continue to say whatever pops into my head, with or without a conscious thought, and every once in a while I'll scribble it down with one of my sharpened pencils. If I happen to scribble something book-worthy, it'll be your job to let me know. You see, it's a regular two-way street, this author-reader relationship. I have an obligation to you, to entertain and enlighten and mildly amuse, and you have an obligation to me, to subsidize my extravagant lifestyle by buying this fucker in the first place. Also, you have to tell me if everything is spelled properly.

With any luck, I'll come up with enough material to justify the senseless killing of all the trees to produce all the paper we'll need to print the millions of books my adoring public will surely demand. And, you'll laugh uproariously at my creative, soulful talent, which will surely be evident on every page.

Another thing I'll need from you on this two-way street: I have some trouble in my everyday, not-writing-a-book life with double meanings, so you'll have to watch out for this, too. A lot of words, you can take them the wrong way, and if you must know I don't *always* mean to offend. I only *sometimes* mean to offend. For example, I might use a perfectly inoffensive phrase, like *lick a problem*, which is what you do when you solve a dilemma. Harmless enough, right? And yet from the lips of the wrong person, taken in just the wrong way, at just the wrong time, a phrase like that can appear lewd or suggestive, and far be it from me to appear lewd or suggestive. Same goes for *blow a chance*, which is what you do when you let an opportunity pass you by. Put a negative spin on that one and you might raise a few eyebrows, or start looking for some prep school WASP named Chance and wondering why he gets so much head. *Come into money . . .* that's another one that might give me some trouble. I could be writing a perfectly innocent sentence about shooting my wad into a pile of cash, and readers might get the wrong idea, so it'll be good to have another set of professional eyes on this thing.

So where was I? Oh, yeah. My book. The bound stack of paper or digital e-file you hold in your hands. Of course, I'm not so full of myself to expect this book to be another *Crime and Punishment.* (Hopefully, it won't feel so long.) (Plus, I hear the ending on that one is kind of a bummer.) My goals are fairly modest, actually. Writers are always saying that when you write an essay or a paper you should have a clear goal in mind. You should have some idea what you want to say, and some idea how to say it. I'm not quite there yet, but I do know this: I want people to read this book and come away thinking it wasn't a waste of their time or money.

I set the bar high, I know, but that's just me. At the very least, I want the book to be the literary equivalent of a slice of pizza and a grape drink. That's all. It might not be a gourmet meal, but it should at least be filling. The drink is just water, sugar and food coloring. The pizza is just okay, but it tastes all right and is somewhat satisfying.

So here's your slice of pizza and grape drink. I hope it doesn't cause violent vomiting.

Clip 'n' Save Joke no. 1 ✂----------------

Two desperately horny guys are stranded on a deserted island with a beautiful woman. At some point, after much begging and pleading, the woman agrees to have sex with them. They've all been stranded on this island for so long that even she is desperate and horny, and so the two men and the beautiful woman start having wild sex in every conceivable position. They go at each other, over and over and over, day after day after day. They do it upside down, front and back, inside out.

Finally, the beautiful woman can't take it anymore. With tears in her eyes she says, "I'm so ashamed about what we've been doing that I'm going to kill myself." And she does. She wraps a rope around her neck, and tosses the loose end over the branch of a tree, and hangs herself.

Two months pass, and one man says to the other, "I'm so ashamed about what we've been doing." The other man says, "You're right. I guess we should bury her."

1

Story of My Life

I've done some research. I'm no slouch. Okay, strike that. Maybe I am a slouch. Certainly, my posture could be a bit better. But before I started writing I did go to the library and ask around. Here's what I found out: the best books of all time usually start with a classic opening scene. Also, the classic opening scene is supposed to give readers the full flavor of the book, and to introduce the main character in an exciting, compelling, memorable way.

So that's what I'm going for here.

First, an observation: people seem to assume that comics get a lot of pussy. This may, in fact, be true. Specifically, people assume that comics get a lot of stripper pussy. This, too, might very well be the case—but what the hell do I know?

Now, I suppose the reason for this type of thinking is that comics and strippers tend to work the same types of fleabag clubs, at all hours of the night, and that we keep seeing each other backstage, where the strippers are probably walking around on their knees, giving blow jobs, while us comics regale them with jokes and impressions and honey-scented semen.

Unfortunately, this has not been my experience, although I once managed to get a stripper's phone number. At the time, I counted this as a career highlight, and it's still up there on my list of all-time accomplishments. I wish I could remember what I said to this woman, what line I used, but the entire transaction has been blocked from my memory. It was always such a torturous thing for me, talking to women, trying to get into their pants.

If there is a hell, and if that's where I'm going, there'll probably be an endless gag reel being played on some big-screen television of me trying to talk to women. It would play all the time. It would start out funny, and then it would quickly become frightening—because, really, it was a whole new trauma, each time out. For all my charm and girth and apparent good looks, I was a disaster at this sort of thing. Ninety-nine percent of the time, I'd get shot down. Once in a while, the woman would look back at me through a fog of smoke and alcohol and say something encouraging like, "Wait, I'm sorry, were you talking to *me*?"

And yet on this one occasion, with this one stripper, the stars aligned and the gods smiled and everything seemed to work as well as it could have worked. Better, even. It's possible the stripper gave me her number by mistake, but I didn't care. All I cared about was that she answered the phone when I called the next day like she was happy to hear from me, which I took as a good sign.

I said, "It's me, Gilbert?"

She said, "Do I know you?"

I said, "Yes, we met last night at the club. You gave me your number. You told me to call."

She said, "And?"

I said, "And this is me, calling."

You'd think I would have prepared something to say, a piece of witty banter to reinforce the fact that I was a brilliant young comedian, fluent in the art of effortless conversation, but I wasn't smart enough to think things through in just this way.

Somehow, she agreed to meet with me. We arranged the time and place. I was terrifically excited, because I'd already seen this woman naked, which was like half the battle. In my head it meant that our getting together and having sex was basically a sure thing, and even if it didn't work out I could go home afterward and jerk off to what I remembered of her tight stripper body.

All was right in my little corner of the world.

Now, all these years later, I wish I could remember the stripper's name. Candy, I think. Or maybe it was Gum.

Somehow, I ended up taking her back to my apartment. I thought, *This is going well.* We started making out, and the whole time all I could think was, *Oh my God! I'm making out with a stripper!*

Over on her side of the couch, all she could think was, *Oh my God! I'm making out with a Jew! I'm so excited! This man killed my Lord!*

Somehow, her clothes started coming off. She was wearing this very sexy stripper-type underwear. I was half-expecting a pair of day-of-the-week granny panties, reminding us that it was Tuesday, but there I was in the middle of a Victoria's Secret catalogue.

Somehow, my clothes started coming off and the stripper

didn't run from the apartment in horror. This, too, I took as a good sign. I wouldn't go so far as to suggest that the stripper was impressed with my physical gifts, but at least she wasn't put off. This was certainly something. Not much, but something. By this point, the young lady was committed, I guess you could say. Or, quite possibly, nearsighted.

Next thing I knew, we were in my bedroom, about to do it doggy-style. These days, when I do it doggy-style with my wife, it's a little different. She plays dead and I beg. But back then, in the full flower and vigor of my youth, this hot, agreeable stripper was on all fours, and it was possible to stand back from the scene and squint and convince myself that she was the one doing the begging. I couldn't believe my luck. My head was ready to explode. Nothing like this had ever happened to me. It was, without question, the single most thrilling moment of my life. It's a wonder I didn't start barking.

And then it was over. Just like that. My stripper friend lifted her butt toward me in a final enticing display, and I congratulated myself yet again for my great good fortune. Then I made my final approach and if I confess here that I managed to hold off for a full second before ejaculating I'd be exaggerating. If you must know, I don't think I made it in past the tip, just an inch or so—which was a shame, really, because I had a whole other inch or so to go in the physical gifts department. I just slipped my cock into her tight little stripper pussy and shot my wad in no time at all. Maybe I managed a meager half-thrust. I was in such a state of bliss and ecstasy I couldn't control myself.

As soon as I came, my stripper friend looked back at me over her naked shoulder with an expression that seemed to be equal parts disgust, disappointment and disregard. Her face was just one big *dis* after another. She said, "You've got to be kidding me, Gilbert. Did you just come?"

(Careful readers will note here that I've chosen the more socially acceptable spelling of the word *come*, as opposed to the more vulgar, more hardcore *cum*. If the subject *cums* up later on in these pages I'll probably do the same, but I can't make any promises. After all, I want this book to be accessible to the widest possible audience. With any luck, it'll be something parents can read to their children, for generations.)

I couldn't think how to answer. I was a little too out of breath and a little too deep into the throes of my short-lived ecstasy to think much of anything, so I just slipped my limp dick from this lovely stripper pussy and slinked off to the bathroom to bask in my own shame. And, to curse myself for not thinking of Ned Beatty in that great ass-raping scene from *Deliverance*. It could have saved me, that scene. If I'd just thought to picture Ned Beatty on all fours in front of me, instead of this hot, young, tight-bodied stripper, I might have lasted a full thrust.

(Or, as an alternative, I could have held on a little bit longer if I was looking at some naked pictures of myself.)

When I returned to the bedroom, I was still walking on air. I approached my new lover, who was still on all fours, only now it was because she was looking for one of her contact lenses. I leaned toward her and whispered hotly into her ear, "Was it as good for you as it was for me?"

It was at this point she gave me "the look"—the look that said, *Yes, I'm a totally hot piece of stripper ass, for now, but in less than a year they'll find my dead body, which by that point will look like it belongs to an eighty-year-old woman, having died from a drug overdose or from being stabbed in the throat by my biker boyfriend. So, you see, I can easily kill you right now and not give it a thought.*

Well, we've all been on the receiving end of that look . . . so I backed off and let my lover be. If there's one thing I know about women, it's when to let them be. God knows, I've had an awful lot of practice.

I called the stripper later to see if she'd like to get together again, but there was a silence on the phone that seemed to suggest she was back to giving me that "look." And so, in a blind panic, I hung up the phone and went about my business.

Okay, so there's my big, sock-o opening. Right out of the gate, you get the full flavor of me and my life so far. It's all right here, in this neat little anecdote. But apparently they want me to write a little bit more, so I'll keep going. Where I'm going, I've got no idea. I'm just making this stuff up as I go along, which people tell me is how most authors go about writing their books, so I'm not too worried. No kidding, they just make this stuff up, or pull it from thin air, or they stick their fingers down their throats and something comes up, and somehow or other everything comes together and starts to look and feel and smell like a book, which is close enough in my book.

(And all this time, I just thought this stuff was written down somewhere.)

Another thing I found out on that ill-advised trip to the library is that a lot of these books start at the beginning. A very good place to start, if you believe Julie Andrews. The writer picks a point in time, and shares a few autobiographical anecdotes, and then things really start moving, so I figure

I'll give that a try. (Hey, at this point, I'm up for anything.)
I'll reach back a couple generations and start with my grandmother. I called her Bubbie. In Brooklyn, it wasn't the most
original name for a grandmother, but in my defense I had no
idea that it was Yiddish for grandmother. I just liked the
name. I liked my Bubbie, too. She used to visit us every
week, and before she came over she always baked some pastries for us. She was well known for her *mandelbrot*, which is
like Jewish biscotti. (If you happen to be a ninety-seven-
year-old Jew, and someone is reading this book to you at the
home, you'll know exactly what I'm talking about.)

As soon as I started ripping open all these Jewish delica-
cies, my Bubbie would go to work on her English. For some
reason, she decided that I would be her helper. She was determined to speak perfect English. All week long, she'd collect newspaper articles and remember the one or two words
she didn't understand. Or she'd hear something on television
that made no sense to her, and make a mental note of it.
Then, as I stuffed my face, she would tell me the word she
didn't understand and ask me the meaning.

In addition to her pastries, my Bubbie also came prepared
with at least one joke she'd heard that week—very often with
a word or two missing, because she didn't understand it. The
one joke I still remember is the only joke she ever told that
was even close to off-color. (Probably that's why I remember
it.) The joke turned on the Yiddish expression *tsuris*, which is
pronounced *tsoo-ris,* and basically means "troubles" or "difficulties." The joke went something like this: *An old Jewish
man is sitting on a train, shaking his head back and forth and crying.
Every once in a while, he puts his face in his hands and says,*

"*Tsuris! Oy, tsuris! Such tsuris!*" *An Irish man walks by and hears the old man's cries and says, "If you have such a sore ass, why don't you go to a doctor?"*

My Bubbie lived to 104, which is probably a little too old to consider a ripe old age, because she had already started to turn. I still say she died young. When I was little, she used to take me by the hand to the neighborhood butcher. She would order brains. This, too, wasn't so original. Lots of Eastern European Jews eat brains, it turns out, but I don't want to scare off my Gentile readers, so let me state for the record that not all Jews eat brains. We do, however, all drink the blood of Christian babies.

Have I mentioned that we were Jewish? Does that come across? A lot of people, they see my act, and the fact that I'm Jewish never enters their minds, which takes me to a true story. On second thought, the story is really more of an aside than a stand-alone anecdote. It's an important distinction, and it's probably in all of our best interests to consider it here, before this book gets away from us. Really, it's more of a space filler than an attempt to advance the story or keep my confused readers turning the pages. As a side note—specifically, as a side note to my aside, which I guess puts us way, way off to the side for the moment—I should mention that most of the stories I plan to share in this book are true, except for the ones that aren't. Even the asides. This one happens to be true. It was 1980. I was a young comic, about to be discovered. I went to a casting call for the new season of *Saturday Night Live*. It was the year the show went from being good and relevant and talked about to when it started to suck. It was also the year that my career went from sucking to being good and relevant, but only for a while. I might write a bit more about *Saturday Night Live* later on, if I need to fill a few pages, but for now I'll tell just enough to set up this story.

(Remember, this is meant to be an aside, and I've read enough book reviews to know that if an aside takes too long to tell it's not really an aside. Then it's more of an *amiddle*, and it gets in the way of the story. That's about the last thing I want to do, get in the way of my story, which is basically how I've tried to live my life as well. I prefer to stay out of the way, off to the side, where I'm less likely to offend.)

Anyway, the show back then was produced by a woman named Jean Doumanian, who happened to be a great friend of Woody Allen. For those of you who aren't familiar with Jean Doumanian's work, she was the type of person who would watch a Marx Brothers movie and say, "Well, Margaret Dumont is good, but why do they need those strange gentlemen running around her?"

It just so happened that Woody Allen himself decided to come down to an NBC screening room one afternoon, to watch the auditions with his good friend Jean Doumanian. Maybe his adopted children were busy that day, with play-dates of their own, so he needed to find something to do. He had his reasons, I'm sure, and it just so happened that I was one of the comedians he just so happened to catch on tape that afternoon. It also just so happened that I was doomed to overuse the phrase *it just so happened*, simply because of this strange confluence of events.

Let's review: there was me, at the *Saturday Night Live* audition. There was Jean Doumanian. And then there was every working comic in New York. All in the same room, trying to impress the hell out of each other. And then, a couple days later, there was Woody Allen and Jean Doumanian and another few influential people crammed into a darkened screening room, reviewing our auditions on videotape, so of course it just so happened that we all came together in just this way.

Woody sat in the back, off to the side, all by himself. All afternoon, he sat and sat. For a comic genius, he could be a pretty stone-faced guy, and here I'm told it's like he was posing for the fifth spot on Mount Rushmore. Comic after comic, audition after audition, this guy didn't say a word. He didn't laugh. He didn't smile. Or so I was told. And then it was my turn. I popped up on screen and went into my act. I did a few voices. Somewhere in the room, I'm almost sure of it, somebody laughed. But not Woody. He didn't laugh. He didn't smile. He just crinkled up his face in an unpleasant way, as if he had just come into close proximity with some turned cheese, and leaned toward no one in particular and gestured toward me and said, "Is he a Navajo Indian?"

True story.

How do I know this is a true story, if I wasn't even there? One word: you can't make this stuff up. (Yes, I know, that's actually six words, but I was never a big fan of counting.) I also know this because one of the *no ones in particular* seated next to Woody Allen told me about it afterward, and for a brief moment I thought about changing my name to something a little more Native American–sounding, like Dances With No Rhythm or Sleeps With His Hands On His Balls.

Truth was, I was about as Navajo as Shelley Fabares. I was Jewish, through and through, although in our house that didn't mean a whole lot. We never went to synagogue. I never had a Bar Mitzvah. We didn't keep kosher or observe the Sabbath. In fact, I'm not so sure I would have known what the Sabbath looked like if it passed me on the street, so how could I observe it? And yet we were Jewish. This alone wasn't so unusual. Where I was born, in Coney Island, it wasn't the most Jewish neighborhood. In other parts of Brooklyn, though, and all over New York, we were a regular plague. Okay, so maybe I'm overstating. We Jews tend to do that, I've heard. Let's just say there were a great many of us, and we were all rather pleased with ourselves. But that's where it ended for me. I enjoyed a nice sour pickle from time to time, or maybe a Hebrew National hot dog, but that was about it.

Some people, they're born Jewish, and they disavow their heritage. Like Sarah Michelle Gellar, the aging teen actress. Nothing against Sarah Michelle Gellar, the aging teen actress, although I don't think she'd mind being mentioned in this context. She could use the publicity. She goes around saying she was born Jewish but she doesn't consider herself a Jew. What's *that* about? I mean, with her nose, she doesn't really have a case, but she keeps at it.

I've never understood people who say they're not a practicing Jew. You never hear a black guy say he's not a practicing African-American. What does it even mean?

Yeah, I'm not a practicing Jew. I buy retail. I never count my change when I leave a store.

My father considered himself an atheist. He identified himself as a Jew, but he was a Jewish atheist. We never really talked about God or religion or eternity around the dinner table. In fact, we never really talked about much of anything, we were so busy stuffing our faces. To my father, being a Jew meant that if the Nazis came back, we'd be loaded into the cars with everyone else. Even Sarah Michelle Gellar would be along for the ride. That would be a small silver lining, if the Nazis ever came back into power. Yeah, it would be terrible, because nobody likes to be persecuted or tortured or on the receiving end of such all-around unpleasantness, but at least we'd get to see Buffy and smile knowingly to ourselves and think, *Aha! I knew she was a Jew. Who did she think she was fooling? And with that nose!*

Of course, we couldn't count on Buffy to kick any sort of ass on our behalf, or help us escape. She'd be standing off to the side, hoping no one would notice her, saying, "I'm sorry, I wish I could help, but my hands are tied. In college, I studied vampires. Vampires, I can slay. But I missed that whole Nazi thing. It's just not my field."

Don't get me wrong, I'd happily add Sarah Michelle Gellar to my list of Jews I'd Like to Fuck, because the fact that she's a self-hating Jew just makes her hotter, and leaves me wanting to drive my stake into her.

What's that you say? You didn't know there was such a list. Oh, indeed. I keep it wrapped up in my mezuzah, for easy reference. I take it out and update it from time to time. Of course, it follows that there is a subcategory to this list— Jews Who'd Consider Fucking Me—but I can't imagine that list would be too terribly long. (You'll notice I'm not including my list of Gentiles I'd Like to Fuck because there's simply not enough room in the book.) Being a Jew, it's only too easy to want to fuck shiksas. The true challenge, for us horny chosen few, is to lust after one of our own. At the top of the list, four out of five rabbis surveyed can agree, is Natalie

Portman, and here most readers are probably scratching their heads or sticking their meaty paws down the front of their pants and saying, "She's Jewish?" Yes, she is—and that's a tribute to her hot, steaming beauty, that you even have to ask. She's so hot you'd almost have to turn down a Gentile for the chance to have sex with her.

(Confession: watching Natalie Portman on Broadway was the only time I've ever jerked off to a production of *The Diary of Anne Frank*. I have, however, jerked off on several occasions to Hal Holbrook's stirring performance as Mark Twain, for those of you keeping score.)

Another hot Jew? Bar Refaeli, the Israeli model. Scarlett Johansson. Jennifer Connelly. Abe Vigoda's wife on *Fish*. The two actresses from *That '70s Show*. They also follow in the goes-without-saying department. Also, Phyllis Diller, another perfectly do-able Jewess, although it's possible I'm over-estimating Phyllis Diller's appeal because she's a comic. In the real world, she'd be the first to tell you, she's not much to look at. But in the subterranean world of stand-up comediennes, she's a regular Marilyn Monroe. And by *regular*, of course, I mean she shits lilacs.

Back to Coney Island, where we were safe from Nazis and vampires for the time being. The most haunting thing about Coney Island was a clown with a whip that kept turning up on the boardwalk, next to the Steeplechase ride. That's just the sort of thing a small, benignly Jewish boy needs to keep him up nights, a clown with a whip. Either one, without the other, and it would have been no big thing, but a clown *and* a whip? It was plainly terrifying. The Steeplechase ride was unsettling enough. There were creepy wooden horses, racing against each other on a rickety wooden track, round and round like on a twisted merry-go-round. And then there were the creepy, hardly toothed carnival types who ran the midway. It was like growing up in the middle of a Fellini movie. A lot of times, I look back on my childhood and wonder if it wasn't all some terrible nightmare, but then I start to think that everyone must have grown up in the shadow of a clown and a whip and a Steeplechase ride. That's normal, right? The subtitles might have tipped me off, but as I've indicated, I wasn't the most observant child.

I went to P.S. Something Or Other. I never could remember the number. Math, counting . . . these just weren't my strong suits. Also, observing and paying good attention. Back then, I didn't exactly have a strong suit. Just regular suits. I was like every other kid on that boardwalk, trying to put my thumb over the hole-punch on my Steeplechase card, so the creepy guy working the ride would give me a free turn. *This*, I realize now, was what it meant to be a practicing Jew. And I was getting good at it!

I cracked my first joke when I was four or five years old. People are still talking about it. (Basically, it's just *me* who's still talking about it, but I'm hoping that once I mention it here it will catch on.) We were at my grandmother's apartment, in Brooklyn. She had a long couch in her living room, and we were all seated on it, waiting for my sister Arlene to take our picture. Arlene was our family photographer, only she took such a painfully long time to set up her shot. Even at four or five years old, I was impatient. Finally, after we had been sitting there a good long while, my entire family across this big long couch, I said, "When's this roller coaster gonna start?"

It wasn't much of a joke, but it got a big laugh. My sister Arlene didn't think it was funny, but my parents and my grandmother thought it was hysterical. It caught them off-guard—a line like that, from a kid like me.

I did my first bit at P.S. Something Or Other. (Comedy historians take note: this Gottfried character doesn't have the best eye for detail—and, for a Jew, he doesn't have the best eye for retail, either.) I was in kindergarten, and my mother used to walk me to school. I was a very shy kid. The routine was the teacher would call out your name, and you were supposed to say "Here!" or "Present!" They called it "Taking Attendance," and it wasn't my best subject. Every day, the teacher would call my name and I'd just sit there. I wouldn't say anything. And the other kids would laugh and laugh, like me not saying anything was just about the funniest thing in the world. Who knows, maybe it was. But then one day, as I was walking to school with my mother, I thought to myself, *Today's the day, Gilbert. Today's the day you'll finally say something when they take attendance.* And underneath that thought it occurred to me this would probably get a big laugh, because it would be such a surprise. I was five or six years old, and already I was working the room, assessing the crowd.

Sure enough, the teacher called my name and I raised my hand and said, "Here!"

Let me tell you, *it killed.* The other kids in the class just went crazy. At Rest Hour, which turned out to be one of my better subjects, they were still talking about it. At Snack Time, another one of my strengths, they were still talking about it. One of my classmates, a hardly Jewish boy named Timothy, did a chocolate milk spit-take that people are still talking about. No one could get over it. Me, out of nowhere, after all this time, announcing myself.

So that was my first bit. My humor was very subtle in those days.

My next big performance came later that year, or maybe it was in first grade. Who can remember? (Comedy historians, take further note: this Gottfried character can't be trusted with the details of his own story.) This time, the teacher was frustrated with a kid who happened to be sitting next to me. He kept turning his head away from the teacher, and couldn't seem to pay attention. These days, they'd send the kid off to the school psychologist and have him tested for Attention Deficit Disorder, but they weren't so sophisticated about these things at the time. Instead, the frustrated teacher just walked past the inattentive student and put a newspaper on his head. She meant it as a joke, I think, but it wasn't a particularly good joke. I thought I could improve on it, so I got up from my seat and pointed to the kid and said, "And those are to-day's headlines!"

Once again, it got a big laugh. Once again, it killed. And it's probably fair to say that my sense of humor hasn't really advanced since that moment. Actually, I still use this line in my act. In fact, I open with it, only now I say, "And those are today's *fucking* headlines."

It's more age-appropriate, don't you think?

Clip 'n' Save Joke no. 2 ✂-----------------

A Jew, an Italian, and a Polish guy are on a deserted island. One day, while they're lying out by the shore, a lamp gets swept up on the sand.

They rub the lamp and a genie pops out. The genie says, "I will grant each one of you a wish."

The Italian says, "I am very lonely. I wish to be back home with my family." The genie waves his hands, there's a puff of smoke, and the Italian is off the island.

Then the Jew says, "I am very lonely. I wish to be back home with my family." The genie again waves his hands, there's another puff of smoke, and the Jew is off the island.

Then the genie turns to the Polish guy and asks for his wish. The Polish guy thinks about it and says, "I am very lonely. I wish those other two guys were back here."

2

Star Power

I'm fascinated by celebrity. Really and truly and utterly fascinated by celebrity. Have been since I was a kid. I used to think it was a great big deal, to meet someone famous. Of course, I usually thought this when I was jerking off to *Barbarella* and wouldn't have minded too terribly much if Jane Fonda walked into my room wearing a hot rubber body suit. That would have been a great big deal, believe me.

There are a lot of people like me, I'm afraid. This is not to say that there are a lot of people jerking off to old Jane Fonda movies—although I suspect that perhaps there are. If they're not, they certainly should be, only not to anything after *On Golden Pond,* because that would just be wrong.

What I mean to say, I guess, is that a lot of people are mesmerized by fame. It's like lifeblood to the huddled masses. We live in a world where even a guy like Osama bin Laden commands our fanaticism. Sure, he might be the most hated man on the planet, especially now that Bernie Madoff has been ass-raped a few dozen times by his fellow inmates, but if Osama bin Laden turned up on a crowded city street one afternoon people wouldn't stone him or call the police or even shout unpleasantries in his direction. No, they'd run up to him and get his autograph, or pose for pictures with him to post on Facebook, or ask him to record an outgoing message for their voice mail. (As if this last would impress anyone, because who the hell would even recognize Osama bin Laden's voice? If he didn't start out saying, "Hi Guys, it's me, Bin," you'd have no idea who the fuck it was.) They'd get him to mug one of those mock, Ali-Frazier publicity poses, with a silly *why-I-oughtta-knock-your-block-off* expression, and they'd consider themselves fortunate to have run into the guy. After that, they'd Tweet to their friends that he's really not so bad after all, just misunderstood. Then Barbara Walters would call, seeking an interview, but Osama's publicist would convince him to hold out for Oprah, even though his client really wants to do the Stern show to talk about how popular Afghani dishes like Quoroot (dried yogurt) and Osh Pyozee (stuffed onions) give him gas.

The first famous person I ever met was Chita Rivera. She was probably fifty at the time. I had a vague idea who she was, and as far as I knew I'd never jerked off to her, so it wasn't the most exciting encounter. She came up to me after one of my shows, when I was just starting out. She said, "Hi, I'm Chita Rivera."

In response, I wanted to say, "Hi, I'm Gilbert. I jerked off to you in *West Side Story*." But I was too shy. Plus, I wasn't so sure this was the case, and I wanted to be accurate. Instead, I said, "Nice to meet you, Chita Rivera."

She told me I looked like one of her nephews or cousins. I told her she looked like Rita Moreno. And that was that. I would have asked her to record an outgoing voice message for me, but I don't think they had answering machines at the time.

This began a long and not entirely successful series of encounters with people much more famous than me. Now, this seemed to be the case every time I met someone who worked in movies or television, where everyone seemed to be much more famous than me, so I never quite managed to narrow the field. Over the years, however, through no fault of my own, I became ever so slightly more famous and recognizable, but it always feels like I'm a notch or two below whoever I'm meeting.

Once, inexplicably, Bea Arthur approached me at some event and said hello. Now, I'm reasonably certain that I never jerked off to Bea Arthur in *Maude,* although her daughter on the show was pretty hot, and I could have been persuaded to join in on a mother-daughter three-way, and I'm also reasonably certain that I never jerked off to Bea Arthur in *Golden Girls,* although Rue McClanahan was nothing to sneeze at.

(Note to self: what does that expression even mean, *nothing to sneeze at*? What would be a good example of something to sneeze at? Or, more to the point, *who* would be a good example of someone to sneeze at? Jimmy Durante, maybe. Karl Malden. Pinocchio . . .)

(Note to reader: you'll notice here that I've inserted the qualifier *reasonably* to soften my certainty about never having jerked off to Bea Arthur, because who among us can be really and truly certain of such a thing? I mean, this is Bea Arthur we're talking about, people. An icon of the small screen! That face! That voice! Those stunning housedresses!)

(Note to editor: ask Gilbert to go easy on these parenthetical inserts, which he has a tendency to overuse.)

(I could go on and on, and at some point I probably will, but right now it's probably best to leave well enough alone. Funny enough, as a side note, I've heard from some of my celebrity friends that *Well Enough* is an affectionate nickname for my penis that's been adopted by women in Hollywood, who also seem to agree that it's probably best to leave Well Enough alone.)

Moving on . . .

Bea Arthur came over to me and said, "Hi, Gilbert. How are you?"

In response, I said the first thing that popped into my head: "I'm fine, Bea, how are you?"

She asked what I was working on, so I told her. Then I asked what she was working on, and she told me. After that there was a long, uncomfortable pause—which is not to be confused with a long, comfortable pause, which is something else entirely. Then, after another few seconds, she stepped back and said, "Do we know each other, or do we just know each other from television?"

I said, "I think we just know each other from television."

Then she walked away.

There's no denying, it was a thrilling encounter—for me, anyway. I can't say for sure if it meant anything to Maude, but it's stayed with me on my all-time list of awkward exchanges with people more famous than me. Again, this designation pretty much applies to every exchange I've ever had with a celebrity, which can't help but turn awkward and uncomfortable.

Here's another one: Harrison Ford. I was appearing on *The Tonight Show,* back before Jay Leno disappeared into prime time—only to return a short while later. *The Aristocrats* had just come out, to reasonably good reviews. I was walking around backstage, and I heard someone say, "Gilbert." So I turned around. That's what I do, when I hear someone say, "Gilbert." I turn around. It usually means someone is trying to get my attention—or, to clear their throat. Either way, if I turn around I have it covered.

Now, Harrison Ford was about as big a celebrity as there was at the time. Indiana Jones. Han Solo. He's still a great star, a hero to horny Amish boys everywhere after the things he did to Kelly McGillis in *Witness*—or, at least, he would be their hero if horny Amish boys were allowed to watch movies. (As it is, they're just going to have to trust me on this.)

Harrison Ford shook my hand and said, "You were very funny in *The Aristocrats.*"

It was music to my ears, a comment like that. No, he didn't *sing* it. As far as I know, the man has no musical talent. *Music to my ears* is just another one of those meaningless expressions. He said something nice, and I was glad to hear it, that's all. Maybe if Marvin Hamlisch was on the show that day there would have been some musical accompaniment, but it was just spoken-word Indy, sotto voce.

(Hmmm . . . I didn't know I spoke Italian. At least I *think* that's Italian. I guess I'm just full of surprises.)

Then Harrison Ford said some other gracious things. I smiled politely, like it was an everyday thing for me, for Han Solo to come up to me backstage at *The Tonight Show* to praise my work—as if what I "do" can even be considered "work" or that it merits any consideration at all. But underneath all these nice things Harrison Ford was saying, I started to feel uneasy. (Frankly, I would have been much more at ease if he *had* broken into song.) Mostly, I couldn't think what I might say in response. Here the great Harrison Ford was saying how funny I was, how he'd just about pissed his pants watching me in this movie, and I didn't want to disappoint him and come across as something less than piss-your-pants funny in real life.

Really, it's a lot of worry, for a guy like me. A lot of times, I think I should have some scripted comeback, for just such a situation. Something I could rehearse. Something that helps me to feel like I'm on my game, instead of like I'm just doing a bad Gilbert Gottfried impression. Other times, I'll just say something sarcastic, and hope it comes across as funny and disinterested. But here, backstage with Harrison Ford, I couldn't think of a single thing to say in response, so I just stood there shuffling my feet until he was finished saying nice things about me. Then I looked at him, blankly, and said, "And who are you again?"

As soon as I said it, I thought, *Okay, that's a little bit funny.* No, it wasn't laugh-out-loud funny, but it was knowing and curious. I don't typically "do" knowing and curious, but it just came out, and once it did I thought, *Maybe Indy will appreciate the subtle nuance of the exchange and deem me worthy of his esteem.*

Or, not—as it turned out.

To this day, I'm pretty sure Harrison Ford had no idea that I was kidding, or that I was going for knowing and curious. He said, "Oh, I'm sorry, Gilbert. I'm Harrison Ford." And then there was a strange pause, during which we each had time to wonder if the name alone was supposed to mean anything, or if he should maybe follow it up with another line or two—like, "I'm an actor. I've been in some movies. Some of them have changed the face of American cinema. Maybe you've seen them." He really seemed to think I didn't know who he was, and that just turned an awkward exchange into something exponentially awkward, which is what happens when you multiply awkward on top of awkward.

And then it got worse. Somehow, I managed to set things right, and indicate that of course I knew who he was, because you'd have to be a complete fucking idiot not to know who Harrison Ford was, but then I followed this one fleeting moment of normalcy by saying something stupid like, "I just came out with a dirty joke DVD. I'll have to send you a copy."

The stupid part about me saying this was that it was *apropos of nothing*. (Another bewildering expression, if you ask me—and here of course I realize that you haven't asked me any such thing, but I believe it helps to follow one bewildering expression with another.) Harrison Ford hadn't just asked, "By the way, Gilbert. Did you just come out with a dirty joke DVD? And, if so, would you be kind enough to send me a copy?" If he had, naturally, my comment would have been *apropos of something*. But Harrison Ford hadn't asked, so my comment just hung there, stupidly, illogically. It had nothing to do with anything, and yet there it was. Then I went home and looked up Harrison Ford's contact information and actually sent the poor man a copy of my DVD, which was a little bit like digging my own grave and jumping inside and asking some people I went to elementary school with and vaguely remembered to piss on me before covering me with dirt.

With one simple trip to the post office, I'd turned an awkward conversation into an awkward transaction, and to this day I regret the whole sorry exchange. One, I regret the joke—*"And who are you again?"*—because it clearly didn't work and I didn't have the balls or the comedy brass to deliver it with conviction. Also, it wasn't that funny. This happens sometimes. A joke alights in your head and seems riotously funny, but then it finds its way out of your mouth and fizzles. It was a simple throwaway line; at best, it was disarming; at worst, weirdly confusing. And two, I regret sending the DVD, because it set it up like I was expecting something in return from this man, who had merely made the mistake of showing me a small kindness backstage at a talk show. That's what happens, whenever someone in the entertainment business sends a book or a script or a something to someone *bigger* in the entertainment business. There's an agenda to it, and a pecking order. If you're like me, on one of the bottom rungs of the celebrity ladder, looking up, it's our way of saying, "Hey, can you make this into something?" If you're on one of the top rungs, looking down, you're saying, "Oh, Christ, what the fuck does this guy want?"

Now, whenever I see a Harrison Ford movie, I can't help but wonder if he ever got the DVD. And, if he did, I wonder if he thought, *I'm such a schmuck. I said hello to this idiot, and now he wants something!*

It ruined *Six Days Seven Nights* for me, I'll tell you that.

(Or maybe it was Anne Heche who ruined it for me. I'll have to get back to you.)

Sometimes, the very best celebrity close encounters are the ones where you don't actually interact with the other person. You hang back like some stalker and find a way to amuse yourself that doesn't involve C batteries or hand lotion. I have a good example of this, somewhere in the dusty corners of my mind. (What, you didn't think I was going anywhere with this?) It's a Julia Roberts–Lyle Lovett–Kiefer Sutherland story, and like every other Julia Roberts–Lyle Lovett–Kiefer Sutherland story it comes with a bit of a setup. Here goes: for years, I'd been making jokes about Julia Roberts and her marriage to Lyle Lovett. It was like manna from comedy heaven, that relationship, and I was really broken up about it when they finally divorced. In fact, it was probably the only time I can remember feeling pain or sadness over the dissolution of a celebrity marriage—only here the pain and sadness was for me.

Why?

Because it meant I couldn't tell any more Julia Roberts–Lyle Lovett jokes in my act. Here's one of my favorites, so you'll know what I was missing: "To think, after all these years, I could have had Julia Roberts. Who knew? I never asked her out because I always thought, *What chance do I have? She's waiting for some incredibly-good-looking guy to come along.* Like every other not-so-incredibly good-looking guy in the world, I didn't have the courage to ask her out, but it turns out that's just what I should have done. What's the worst thing she could have said to me? '*No, Gilbert, I'm sorry. You seem like a nice-enough guy, but you have a normal-shaped head. Maybe if you could just lie down with your head at the foot of an elevator and have the door slam against it for a few hours . . . ' "*

People went crazy for that joke, and now I'd have to retire it, so of course I was distraught over their breakup. You'd be distraught, too, if you'd gone to the trouble of writing such a beguilingly brilliant bit. And for a while I was reluctant to give up on the bit entirely, so I found a way to work it into the act and put it in context and make it still seem relevant, but it was always such a long way to go for a bit. Personally, I like a bit that just kind of sneaks up on you, not one you have to go looking for, because every once in a while I'd lose my way and wind up in the middle of an ill-conceived joke about Broderick Crawford, so at some point I stopped even bothering.

But I kept thinking of Julia Roberts—again, like every other not-so-incredibly-good-looking guy in the world. I followed her career. I closed my eyes and imagined her going down on me. In a room filled with pillows and swimsuit models and, strangely, small kitchen appliances. I looked for opportunities to make jokes about her, and maybe make myself feel a little bit better about being so much less attractive than the misshapen-headed Lyle Lovett that she would never even consider going out with me. Or down on me. Or even just being in close proximity to me.

And then, just when I was feeling so low it appeared I might never write a good, mean-spirited, beguilingly brilliant celebrity joke again, fate smiled down upon me with a close encounter punch line to my Julia Roberts woes. It was almost enough to jump-start the entire genre. You see, people forget that before she threw in with Lyle Lovett, Julia Roberts nearly married Kiefer Sutherland, who I believe was the love child of Elliott Gould and Donald Sutherland. Like Julia Roberts, Kiefer Sutherland was a hot young actor at the time, a guy who was actually good-looking, in a rugged, über-masculine, non–Gilbert Gottfried sort of way. But if you believed the tabloids Julia Roberts broke Kiefer Sutherland's heart just as they were headed to the altar—and why wouldn't you believe the tabloids? It's not like they've ever gotten anything *wrong*.

Anyway, it worked out that one of Julia's movies was playing on my flight to Los Angeles, and it further worked out that Kiefer Sutherland himself was seated in the row directly in front of me.

Again, pure, sweet manna from comedy heaven—and at an altitude of 30,000 feet, we were that much closer to heaven, so the manna was also oven-fresh.

Now, here's where things took an interesting turn. The stewardess got on the plane's loudspeaker system and announced that the movie was about to begin and that she would be coming down the aisle soon with headphones for passengers interested in watching. And, she added, she would appreciate it if everyone would please close their window shades so that we could all fool ourselves into thinking we were sitting in a darkened movie theater instead of careening through the skies at some ungodly rate of speed.

Well, as far as good old Kiefer was concerned, the stewardess might as well have asked us to shit gravy—and then crack the window a bit in consideration of the other passengers.

A couple minutes later, the stewardess stopped at Kiefer Sutherland's row, and asked in her most professional, hostess-y voice if he would like a set of headphones.

"What's the movie?" Kiefer Sutherland asked.

"Julia Roberts in *Runaway Bride*," the stewardess answered— quite reasonably, she probably thought—and at this Kiefer Sutherland merely turned his head and looked out the window. How perfect was that? The comedy gods were smiling on me that day, dear reader, and not because I'd been gifted the chance to see a hackneyed and formulaic Julia Roberts movie. Not at all. The real, everlasting gift of comedy gold was that I was seated directly behind Kiefer Sutherland, as he himself sat in the uneasy crosshairs of his private and public lives. I believed this was what poets have referred to as delicious irony, and I chose to imagine that Kiefer Sutherland made a silent vow to himself that there was no fucking way he would close his shade and darken the cabin to enhance everyone's viewing enjoyment of his ex-fiancée's charade of a farce of a film that put his private heartbreak on public display, but it's possible he just took a nap.

For the time being at least, I was a happy little comedian, and the rest of the flight passed without incident. Really, the time just flew by. It's like we were up in the air or something.

It's a strange business, this celebrity business—but like it or not, accept it or not, I've managed to fit myself into it, even if I'm only sitting one row behind it and can only see the back of its head, like I was on that flight to Los Angeles. Like Kirstie Alley squeezing into last season's bikini, I've fit myself into it. Like Valerie Bertinelli buttering her thighs to slip into something more comfortable, I've fit myself into it. And it never ceases to amaze me, the strange dance that happens when I run into someone I'm supposed to know in show business—because we once sat on the same dais at a roast, or waited in the same green room for our turn on some soundstage. Or maybe somebody I worked with on some movie at one point worked with this other somebody on some other movie.

It doesn't matter where we happen to be, or how famous we are, or how famous we *think* we are, we fit ourselves into each situation like we were born to it. And—invariably, unavoidably—we're drawn to each other. Like the time I ran into Howie Mandel at a radio station in Chicago. He was making the rounds, promoting his book about being a germaphobe. I was out promoting the dirty jokes DVD I couldn't interest Harrison Ford in turning into a big-budget movie. We talked for a bit at the station, between our interview segments, and as Howie left he told me where he was staying and suggested I stop by afterward.

This alone wasn't unusual. I'd known Howie for years. We weren't exactly friends—he'd never invite me to his kid's Bar Mitzvah, except possibly to wait tables—but we ran in some of the same circles. When you work in stand-up, you tend to follow the careers of other people who work in stand-up. You know all the same people, the same places. It's kind of like the way everyone assumes that all black people know each other, only in this case we do. Kind of, sort of. Especially if we're Jewish. Then there's a secret handshake, too.

Anyway, I did my interview and told the cleaned-up versions of some of my dirty jokes. Then I went to see Howie at his hotel. Here again, not so unusual, right? We can ignore each other in New York or Los Angeles, but since we'd run into each other on the road, in the middle of nowhere, we had to make this little extra effort to get together, only it just so happened that I was suffering with a really bad cold. I was coughing and sneezing like crazy, and it never once occurred to me how deliciously ironic it was that I would now be doing my coughing and sneezing next to one of the biggest germaphobes of our time.

(Is there any other kind of irony, *really?*)

Let me put this in terms you can easily understand: Howie Mandel is the kind of guy who would ask a girl to gargle with Purell before giving him a blow job. He's over-the-top about this stuff, but I didn't think anything of it just yet. I was too focused on the particulars of our celebrity dance. We found a nice little seating area in the hotel lobby and sat down, and I started coughing almost as soon as we started talking. I was having these uncontrollable fits of coughing, just hacking and gurgling and sounding like I was about to spit up blood.

Howie recoiled, like he'd just heard a gunshot. He said, "Wait a minute, Gilbert. Are you *sick?*" He looked at me like I'd just taken a big, hot, steaming shit, right in the middle of the hotel lobby. Or, like I'd just taken a swig from a bottle of Purell and was about to go down on him.

I said, "I have this cough. I can't seem to shake it." Then I coughed some more, and attempted a full body shudder meant to indicate that I was trying to shake it.

He said, "What the fuck is the matter with you?" Then he moved over to the far edge of the sofa where we were sitting and turned away from me. I think he even covered his face with a scarf. He was like a kid in kindergarten, deathly afraid of catching my cooties.

I said, "Oh, that's brilliant, Howie. That's very mature, and scientifically sound. Of course, my germs can't make a left turn and find you facing away from me, all curled up like that in the corner of the couch. They can only go forward, in a straight line." Then I put on my most annoying, most sarcastic voice (as opposed to my merely somewhat annoying, somewhat sarcastic voice) and said, "You're perfectly safe now."

He said, "Fuck you, Gilbert."

The great part about this visit with Howie Mandel was that we continued to sit and talk in this way for a while longer. He asked about my family. I asked about his. He asked about my career. I asked about his. And yet the whole time he was curled up in his corner of the couch, facing away from me, talking into his scarf, while I was doing what I could to steer my germs directly onto his person.

And then at some midpoint in this weird, sick exchange, it occurred to me . . . the answer to one of life's great questions: no, Rue McClanahan might have been nothing to sneeze at, but Howie Mandel?

Clip 'n' Save Joke no. 3 ✂------------

Two snails are walking down the street when they are attacked by a turtle. A short while later, a policemen arrives at the scene. "Can you tell me what happened?" the police officer says.

"I don't know," the first snail replies. "It all happened so fast."

3

Not Living up to My Potential

I don't like to talk about my personal life. It's too personal. Also, a part of me thinks my personal life is nobody's business. Another part can't imagine why anyone would even want to know about this stuff. However, I guess I could share a little bit of it with you, dear reader, but only if you promise not to tell anybody. You see, I've spent all this time building all these walls and closing myself off from all these memories and feelings that I'd hate to undo all that good work just to sell a couple books. That sort of thing would be beneath a stand-up guy like me, don't you think? Besides, I'm not really in touch with my memories and feelings—at least, not enough to write about them. We used to be in touch, but we had a falling-out. We're working through a few things.

But this is a book, so it's not all about me. Yeah, I know, it's *my* book, so you'd think it might be all about me, but you'd be wrong. As it happens, it's also about this character I once saw in a movie, who seemed to have his shit together. He was a dashing young man, fairly oozing with charm and warmth and good cheer. Me, I'm just fairly oozing. This other character, he had women and money and cars. Me, I just have dick jokes and some loose change and I can some-times tell the difference between a car and a bus. Together we make an interesting pair.

Okay, so let's just say this is the part of the book that's based on my life. It's not *about* my life, but it's based on it. It's like that line you sometimes see on movie posters, "Inspired by a true story." It means a whole bunch of stuff is made up. The way it works is I think back to something that actually happened, in such a way that I'm inspired to stretch the truth, to embellish, to exaggerate. Basically, to lie. Only here my stories are not exactly inspiring, although there may have been some perspiration involved. It's not quite the same thing, I know, but I thought I'd mention it.

Here are a couple half-truths and distorted memories from my childhood. I'll leave it to you, dear reader, to figure out which is which. Let's start with my father, who served in the military in World War II. He was a Nazi officer, it turned out. (Who knew?) He masterminded the Third Reich. (Again, a big surprise to us Gottfrieds, who were led to believe all along he had been working on the First Reich, which of course at the time would have been known as merely the Reich, since there was no reason to line them up and start counting just yet.)

Actually, let me amend that last misstatement: my father masterminded the Final Solution. That sounds so much bet-ter than being the guy behind all those Reichs, but you can't really blame him; it wasn't really his fault; he was angry at his accountant at the time.

Now, I'm afraid I must put these proceedings on pause for a bit to let you in on a curious exchange between me and my editor. When he read the first draft of the manuscript, he scribbled in the margins that these last few paragraphs about Nazis and the Final Solution didn't really work for him. I couldn't make sense of his handwriting, so I called and asked him to read it to me, and after he did I couldn't make sense of his point. I thought, *Oh, the Third Reich didn't really work for you, huh? So sorry to hear that. Perhaps we can go back and try again. Maybe we can get it right this time.*

We went back and forth on this, in phone calls and e-mails, until it was finally agreed that we would let those earlier paragraphs stand as originally written. The kicker came when my editor threw up his hands in exasperation and sent me an e-mail of surrender. I knew he'd thrown up his hands because he told me later he had to type with his elbows.

(Confession: I know how difficult this can be, typing with your elbows. I've tried to do it myself on several occasions— mostly when I was looking for porn on the Internet and my hands weren't exactly free.)

He wrote, "Do whatever the fuck you want, Gilbert. You're the legendary comedian."

I sent him back an e-mail, apologizing sincerely for having ruined the Holocaust for him. "Trust me," I wrote. "It won't happen again. NEVER AGAIN!"

When my father wasn't campaigning for a new world order, he liked to work with tools. He was very handy—which in turn came in handy with respect to his thriving Final Solution business. He had a hardware store, and he knew how to use everything he sold. This must have been a good quality in a hardware store owner, although you'd never have known it to look at his business ledger. (Also, you'd never have guessed he even *had* a business ledger.) He had drawers and drawers of nails and screws and nuts and bolts, of every conceivable size. He was a regular Mr. Fix-It. He could break open walls, rewire an electrical system and re- pair the plumbing. Sometimes he did these things in our neighbors' apartments, and he'd have to work very quickly, before the police showed up.

At this point, most readers are probably asking them- selves, "Gee, Gilbert, with a hands-on, take-charge father like that, how did you turn out to be such a pussy?"

Well, I have my mother to thank, if you must know. Or, to blame—not that she was in any way responsible, but I learned early on that someone has to take the blame for every short- coming or failing in your life, and if you can't blame a Jewish mother then who can you blame? And, as long as we're point- ing fingers, there was quite a lot I could hold against my mother. At a time when most women got married and kept house, my mother actually went to college and earned her degree. Then she got married and kept house. She raised me and my two older sisters in a cramped apartment, directly over my father's hardware store, and every once in a while she would remind us she had a college degree.

Now readers are probably saying, "Oh gee, Gilbert. Let me rephrase the question. With a hands-on, take-charge fa- ther like that, and a strong, independent woman for a mother, how did you turn out to be such a *fucking* pussy?"

Another good question, I must admit. And here again, I have no good answer, but that won't keep me from distract- ing you with an irrelevant aside. Here goes: back then, when my parents were young and just starting out, you didn't have an option to be a pussy.

(Note to filmmakers: perhaps it's time to permanently retire the phrase "Failure is not an option," unless you happen to be making a movie about a census taker who takes his job way too seriously, in which case the phrase could be reasonably made to apply.)

(A follow-up note to filmmakers: "Not on my watch!" is another tired line that should be banned from all future productions, and as long as I'm on it let's make it against the law in Hollywood for a character to recognize that he or she is an unusual situation and to remark that they're not in Kansas anymore.)

Back to me and my plain, nonpussy existence: there were no Mommy & Me groups, no playdates, no DVDs like *Baby Einstein,* which as far as I know give you valuable tips on how to be . . . well, a baby Einstein. For that, in my day, we just went to our snake oil salesman.

We kids were left on our own a lot. We learned to amuse ourselves, which in my case turned out to pay dividends in the jerking off department, where I soon demonstrated a certain degree of proficiency. My parents were too busy to chase after us. That, or they couldn't be bothered. Or maybe their interests lay elsewhere. My father was always downstairs, working, but I never saw any customers in his store. For all his expertise, for all his nuts and bolts, for all his abilities with a hammer and screwdriver . . . every time I went in there, the place was empty. I don't know why he even had locks on the doors, other than to advertise the fact that he sold them inside. You could have had a girl lying next to an open cash register with her legs hanging open and no one would have walked into that store, which was called "Gilbert's Father's Hardware Store," because even then my family was cashing in on my name—although, looking back, having a girl with her legs open lying next to the cash register would have been a useful accessory for my developing skills as a world-class masturbator.

My father wasn't much of a businessman, but he could sniff an opportunity. Literally. For a while when I was growing up, young people in New York City were into sniffing glue. Nowadays, kids experiment with all kinds of illegal drugs, but in my day all it took was a tube of model airplane glue to get high. It was a much more wholesome brand of drug abuse, and it was all the rage.

(Ah, life was so much simpler back then . . . just ask Norman Rockwell.)

You'd see kids walking down the street in the middle of the day with their noses pressed into brown paper lunch bags and think for a moment they were inhaling some exotic new blend of tuna fish sandwich. Or, they'd be sitting on a stoop, passing a bag back and forth, and you'd wonder how many bites there could be in one little tuna fish sandwich, that so many people could share it.

As a result of all this glue sniffing and apparent tuna fish sandwich sharing, there was an ordinance passed in New York City restricting the sale of model airplane glue. Under the new law, you couldn't sell model airplane glue unless you were also selling a model as part of the same transaction. It was a stupid law, really, because it didn't account for those actual model airplane hobbyists who might have already purchased their model and simply run out of glue, but my father wasn't the sort of businessman to question a new local ordinance. He only cared that he could make money from it, so he dusted off the cheapest model airplane kit he could find on the back of one of his shelves. In fact, it was the only model airplane kit in the store, and it had been there forever. It was a Wright Brothers model, and if I'm not mistaken it was actually made by the Wright Brothers.

Like every other item in the store, my father had pretty much given up on the thought of selling this one model airplane kit, but then this ordinance happened and it was a regular Christmas miracle—except for the fact that it was nowhere near Christmas at the time. This one model airplane kit was so cheap my father could price it for about a quarter. Also, it was so cheap that if you bothered to actually build the model and then stood back to admire your handiwork, it would fall apart if you looked at it too closely. Whatever wood there is in nature that's flimsier than balsa wood, that's what they used for these kits. He put this one model airplane kit next to the rack where he kept the modeling glue, hoping the nutty neighborhood kids would reach for it so they could go off and get high without breaking the law. The model was like a necessary ingredient, the key to the whole transaction, but he knew the kids didn't give a shit about the model. He knew all they'd care about was that it only cost a quarter.

But get this: the first group of kids who bought the cheap model tossed it in the trash as soon they left. My father found it in the garbage can by the side of the store later that afternoon. This was the Christmas miracle part of the story. The kids hadn't even opened it, so my father picked it up and brought it back inside so he could sell it again. And again. It got to where the kids would leave the store and he'd count to three. Then he'd go outside and reclaim the unopened kit. Over and over, he did this. For years, this was our major source of income, all these quarters, until the neighborhood kids found some other way to get high and my father was stuck once again with this one cheap kit, which I believe he finally took as a tax deduction.

He was ahead of his time, my father, one of the original recyclers. And a regular entrepreneur. Some kids, they get to walk around the neighborhood boasting that their fathers were in the airline industry, or that they worked at the airport, but my father the model airplane magnate was in a different end of the business. The lower-than-balsa-wood end.

I don't want to give the impression that my father played fast and loose with the law in his hardware store, because that certainly wasn't the case. There was nothing fast about him, just loose. In fact, there was one time when he was so completely *not fast* that the law caught up to him. Specifically, it caught up to his brother, my Uncle Seymour, who ran the store with my father. Why you needed two people to run a store that was barely a one-man operation was beyond me, but they were partners. And it was a good thing, too, because the police came by one day looking for illegal merchandise. It happened to be a day when my father was out of the store, probably scouring the city for unopened model airplane kits. The police had received a hot tip that my father and uncle were selling party poppers. Remember party poppers? They were little plastic champagne bottles, with a string hanging from the top where the cork was meant to be. You'd pull the string and the thing would "pop" open and spit confetti all over the place. Fun for the entire family and all that.

Well, the cops told Uncle Seymour that it was against the law to sell this novelty item. (The hot tip, it turned out, was the fact that my father and uncle had thought to display these items in the window—a misguided attempt at marketing, it turned out.) The cops said the poppers were some sort of illegal firearm, and they dragged poor Uncle Seymour from the store in handcuffs. Really. Okay, maybe not *really*, but this was how Uncle Seymour always told the story. He liked to embellish, probably because he wanted my father to feel bad for being out of the store that day. In any case, Uncle Seymour wound up spending the day in jail. Really. Okay, okay . . . maybe not *really*, but he was there for a couple hours, which was more than enough time for him to bend for the soap in just the wrong way.

Despite his run-ins with the law, my father the drug dealer and illegal firearms merchant was a hard worker. He was almost always at the store when I was growing up. In this way, he was like everyone else. Fathers weren't around much in those days. They were always working. Not like today, when they're supposed to be around all the time, starting in the delivery room. This is a disgusting new development, if you ask me. It's even pretty disgusting if you don't ask me. Speaking personally, and from the heart, which means you should probably put your ear to my chest if you care to make out what I'm saying, I miss the old days when expectant fathers rolled up their sleeves and paced back and forth in the hospital waiting room, loosening their ties and smoking cigarettes and waiting for their babies to be born so they could get back to work. At least, that's how I *think* it used to happen, although it's possible I might have gotten this from an *I Love Lucy* episode. (Or was it *Dick Van Dyke*? I can't be sure.)

To be clear, my father wasn't in the delivery room when I was born. I don't think my mother was there, either. She was working at the time.

We didn't have a lot of money when I was growing up, but that didn't keep my parents from wanting to indulge us with some of the finer things in life. Money isn't everything, you know, even when it might appear to be *most* things.

(Note to *goyim* readers: not every Jew who grew up in Brooklyn was rich. And as long as I'm on it, here's another note: fuck you. That's all. Whether or not you assumed we were rich, if you're a *goyim*, fuck you. But keep reading, and tell your friends to buy the book.)

Okay, now that I've gotten that bit of unpleasantness out of the way, I'll share another childhood memory. This one is mostly true, and the parts I've made up are mostly inconsequential. One summer, my father decided we should all go away on vacation, so he rented a bungalow in Brighton Beach. Now, if you know anything at all about Brooklyn, you'll know that Brighton Beach is about a five-minute walk from Coney Island, but this was my father's idea of getting away from it all and making a family memory. (It's possible he got this idea from Oprah, but she was still in preschool at the time and I don't think her show had gone national.) We packed up our suitcases and threw everything into our beat-up old car and in less than two minutes we arrived at our bungalow. The whole way there, I sat in the backseat and kept asking, "Are we there yet?" I think I might have even thrown up, but that's just me and long car trips. To this day, if you pick me up in your car and offer me a ride around the block, you'll do well to put down some newspapers on the backseat, just to be safe. Actually, it's probably better for both of us if you don't offer me a ride at all, because the last thing you need is a motion-sick Jew and my cardiologist tells me I could probably use the exercise so I might as well walk.

We pulled up in front of our rented bungalow and spilled out of the car and my father said, "Okay, everyone. Let's have a fun vacation."

That vacation turned out to be a fiasco. The weather was lousy, so we packed up and went home.

Another summer, my parents sent me off to a Jewish camp in upstate New York. I don't remember the name, but it rhymed with Auschwitz. (Also, mostly true.) I think we were served three meals a week, which was plenty, believe me. I still have my old camp T-shirt somewhere. It's faded with the years, but you can still make out the camp colors—smoke and ash. And you can still read the message beneath the camp's spirited hammer-and-sickle-and-swastika logo. It says, "I survived the camp." Only in my case I barely made it through a single session. My father made it through World War II, and I couldn't handle one week of sing-alongs. (This might be another instance of delicious irony, but it still leaves a bad taste.) That should tell you something, and what it tells you is this: I hated camp. With a passion. Which worked out well, because the other kids in my cabin also hated me. Also, with a passion. I don't think there has ever been so much passion passed around among a group of eight-year-old boys.

The camp was run by a couple of Jews who thought it would be worthwhile to devote an entire day of activities to honoring those who died during the attacks on Hiroshima and Nagasaki. I never understood why this was more meaningful to our camp directors than honoring the victims of Pearl Harbor, say, or the victims of the German concentration camps that seemed to bear a passing resemblance to our own little hellhole, but I was eight and I didn't have it in me to question authority. And so we honored the fallen Japs. It was a politically incorrect time, so we ran through the woods with our eyelids taped down. This was our way of showing respect. Then we made lanyards. Then we hiked into the woods so the mountainfolk could rape us.

It was like *Deliverance,* only with bug spray.

(Yeah, yeah . . . I know. That makes two *Deliverance* jokes, and we're not even halfway through this thing, but that should pretty much cover us, here on in.)

Which reminds me . . . why is it that Jews play into all these offensive stereotypes when we have something to celebrate or commemorate? It's innate to our species, I guess. On Hanukkah, we give each other chocolate coins. Whose idea was that? Jews running hither and yon with sacks of money, chocolate or not, doesn't exactly do much to dispel the notion that we're a money-grubbing lot. (And when was the last time you ran hither and yon, anyway?) You don't see Asians taping down their eyelids on their holidays, unless it's at Camp Auschwitz in the Catskills, on Hiroshima Day. You don't see African-Americans walking around in blackface, eating watermelon and singing minstrel tunes. And on Irish holidays, the Irish don't go running around, drinking themselves shit-faced and getting into fights in the street for no apparent reason and then puking their guts out in between parked cars . . . oh, wait a minute. Forget I said that.

It wasn't exactly a formative experience, my brief time at camp, but it was an experience. I never had to swim out to a raft in the middle of a lake, or go canoeing, or hike up some godforsaken peak only to turn around and come right back down, although I did participate in the camp's arts 'n' crafts program. The camp directors, for all their backwoods, backwards thinking, were ahead of their time in this one area. They offered a class in body art, so we all got tattoos. Unfortunately, there wasn't a lot of artwork to choose from, so we were encouraged to burn our camp identification numbers into our forearms as a means of expressing ourselves. Plus, they had that nice mountainfolk raping activity, so we could experience the wilderness in all its splendor and express ourselves in nature. I think I even came home with a nice case of poison sumac on my sphincter, but that's a whole other story.

(Technically, this still counts as an extension of that second *Deliverance* joke, *delivered* just a few paragraphs earlier. It's just that sometimes, in the comedy business, you can wring an extra few drops of funny from a routine a beat or two after the punch line, which is what I'm trying to do here.)

School offered its own brand of childhood trauma. There was no ass raping that I can recall, but I was upbraided on more than one occasion—and, trust me, you haven't suffered until you've been upbraided by a representative of the Board of Education of the City of New York. Speaking personally again, and once more from the heart, I would have much preferred an upbraiding from the Catskills mountainfolk to the special brand of interaction they offered instead, and possibly even to the special brand I had to stamp onto my forearm, but I can't really complain. After all, I did get that T-shirt out of the deal. And I still have all of my old report cards, to memorialize my extra-efforts in the classroom. (This is another one of those "true" parts, I'm afraid.) I don't know why I saved them, but I take them out from time to time, and reconsider my options. Someday, I suspect, I'll donate them, along with my other important papers, to some institution of higher learning. It'll probably be to one of those schools that advertise on late-night television, but still . . .

One of my elementary school teachers, Mrs. Coulborn, wasn't too impressed with my work ethic. She wrote, "Gilbert exerts very little effort and concentration. He seems to dream in class and does not review the necessary information."

On another report card, a teacher named Mrs. Sobel wrote, "He is not doing well. Please come in to see me."

(Those two words, *see me*, were perhaps the most dreaded two words in the annals of public schooling—and if I had to make an uneducated guess, which I'm afraid is the only kind I'm equipped to make, I'd say *annals* ran a close third.)

One of the best things about these old report cards was the "Parent Comment" section on the back. At the time, I probably didn't think it was so wonderful, but after all this time it's nice to have a record of my mother interacting with my teachers. (It's also useful for legal purposes, I'm told, to be able to produce even this meager paper trail to demonstrate that my parents took an interest in my education.) Most parents simply signed the report card, which we underachieving children had to return to the school the next morning to prove to our teachers that our parents had been given the full measure of our underachievements. However, there was also a section for the parent to share a note or a comment. Remember, this was back in the stone age of two-way communication between parents and teachers. Parents couldn't e-mail their child's teacher, or leave a voice mail, or post threatening messages on their Facebook page. They could only write a short note or comment in the tiny space on the back of the report card . . . and my mother certainly did her part.

On one report card, my mother summed up my academic performance with a phrase I have often thought of displaying on a theater marquee, outside one of my comedy shows: "I agree that Gilbert needs to learn how to work," she began, responding to Mrs. Coulborn's report card. "Too much verbalizing just puts a blanket of words over gaps in actual knowledge."

(Note to editor: how about that for a title? "A Blanket of Words over Gaps in Actual Knowledge." Works for me. The bonus here is that there's a nice symmetry, granting naming rights to my mother for my first book. After all, she didn't do such a bad job naming me. I could have been a Bernie or a Milton or an Akmed, and then where would we be?)

(Note to reader: do me a favor and flip back to the cover. If "A Blanket of Words over Gaps in Actual Knowledge" doesn't appear as the title, you'll know who wears the pants in this writer-editor relationship. It's just one editorial battle after another with this guy. Also, as long as you're flipping back to the cover, check to see if there's a picture of me and let me know if I'm wearing pants.)

Another teacher, whose name I can't make out and can no longer recall, thought it was appropriate to criticize my handwriting. This, I would later learn in an odd, inexplicable moment of concentration in high school, was known as a paradox. "I thoroughly recommend he be in bed by 9:00 p.m.," this teacher wrote. "He falls asleep in class." At least, that's what I can make out, although with his poor penmanship I suppose it's possible that what the teacher *really* wrote was, "Never before in my middling career in education have I come across such a brilliant, inventive mind as Gilbert's. Surely, if he gets enough rest, and gets to bed each night by 9:00 p.m., he will grow up to be a comic genius."

And still another teacher, the fortunately named Miss Goldfinger, marked me with straight Fs, which in my school stood for Fair. I was like the poster child for slightly below average academic performance, but I did earn a couple of Us, for Unsatisfactory, in Spelling, Handwriting and Gym. In my defense, I knew it was only a matter of time before someone invented spell-check, before computers replaced pens and pencils, and before I reached the stage in my development where the only physical activity that mattered would be masturbating—one area, as I have indicated, where I could certainly hold my own.

The last I heard of Miss Goldfinger, she had gotten into a bit of a tiff with Sean Connery. As I understood it at the time, things didn't work out too well for her on that score.

Now, I don't want you readers thinking my grade school career was an unmitigated bust. It was merely a mitigated bust. (Personally, I don't know what this means, but it sounds good.) I seemed to show a certain talent for art, which was something—not a whole hell of a lot, mind you, but something. Quite a few of my teachers commented on my ability to draw, and on my active imagination. Just what I was actively imagining, I cannot say with any certainty all these years later, although if I had to bet I'd say it had something to do with monsters. You see, before my deep and abiding interest in not getting laid, I developed a deep and abiding interest in monsters. Movie monsters, mostly. I read all the movie monster magazines, and I had my firm opinions on who was the best Dracula, who was the best werewolf, who was the best Frankenstein monster. (For the record, it was Bela Lugosi, Lon Chaney, Jr., and Boris Karloff.)

My mother was only too happy to see me take an interest in . . . something. Up until this time, she worried I would have a hard time making a living with my hands in my pants and my head up my ass. I was young, and I suppose there was still hope for me, but my mother liked it when she had something to worry about. She signed me up for an art class at the Brooklyn Museum, where it turned out I had a talent for papier-mâché. At least, I didn't suck at it, and it seemed to go well with my active imagination. I started making these papier-mâché monster puppets, which I guess is what you do when you discover you have a talent for papier-mâché and a deep and abiding interest in monsters. They were actually pretty good, and before long I developed a whole puppet show to go with them. The story wasn't much, but I spent a lot of time on the special effects. For one dramatic show-down scene in my acclaimed production of *Dracula*, I cut an ice cream stick in half to use as a stake, which I planned to drive through the heart of my papier-mâché vampire. One half of the stick was its regular color, and the other half I painted red. For the first part of the scene, where one puppet rushes the vampire puppet, I used the regular-colored stick. Then, after I stabbed the vampire puppet repeatedly, I with-drew the red half of the stick from beneath the vampire's cape, which was really an old black kerchief I'd borrowed from my mother's closet.

It was a clever sleight of hand, meant to show that the vampire puppet had been stabbed and that the stake was now covered in blood, and the audience seemed to really appreci-ate it. Of course, when I say *audience*, I should probably men-tion that I'm referring only to my mother and father and two sisters. I would have invited some of the neighborhood kids to one of my performances, but I didn't know any.

Another special effect: for a papier-mâché version of *Jekyll and Hyde,* I prepared a few Dixie cups as props. During the scene where Dr. Jekyll is meant to be in his laboratory mix-ing some new formula, I poured water from one Dixie cup into another cup where I had placed an Alka-Seltzer tablet, which of course started to fizz and bubble.

Once again, the audience was thoroughly entertained. I might go so far as to suggest that they were *wildly* enter-tained, but I'm afraid this would be overstating. Let's just say they were *mildly* entertained, and leave it at that.

After one performance, in fact, my mother came up to me and patted me on the head and said, "That's nice, Gilbert."

Then she told me to clean up after myself. In our apartment, that was the equivalent of a rave review.

To this day, after every show, I wait patiently for a kind older woman to approach me backstage and pat me on the head and say, "That's nice, Gilbert," and then tell me to clean up after myself.

Hey, it could happen.

Clip 'n' Save Joke no. 4 ✂----

A woman is giving birth. The father walks into the delivery room, and the doctor says sadly to both of them, "I'm sorry to tell you that your son's birth didn't go as planned. The good news is he's healthy and smiling. The bad news is he's only a head."

This was a devastating development for the couple, but they raised their son the head with love and affection. They sent him to school. They sent him to camp. He received a good education. He proved surprisingly popular with girls—because, after all, who doesn't like good head?

Eventually, the young head graduated from college, and soon after his parents received a surprising phone call. By some great good fortune, a young man had recently passed away at the hospital, after leaving his body to science. He had been a vibrant, healthy young man—a college athlete, it turned out.

By some great coincidence, it was the head's birthday, so the news was especially meaningful. After all these years, there was now an appropriate match for a transplant. They could put their son's head on this young man's college athlete body, and he could finally live an active, normal life. It was a regular Christmas miracle, only it wasn't Christmas. It was just a birthday. Still, it was an amazing gift, and the parents were terribly excited to see their son the head to tell him the good news. His head would be attached to the body of a strong young weight lifter and all would be right with their world, at long last.

The parents were overjoyed. There were tears streaming down their faces when they tried to tell their son the head their miraculous news. The father couldn't get the words out fast enough. "Son," he said, "we have something wonderful to tell you. You're about to receive the greatest birthday gift of your entire life."

To which the son said, "Oh, not another fucking hat?"

4

Don't Forget to Tip Your Waitress

I had no choice but to go into show business. No other business would have me—and, frankly, there have been times when those on the receiving end of my show business transactions might have preferred it if I'd chosen another line of work, like taxidermy or middle management. And yet here I am, making a go of it, even though I'm not entirely sure what that expression means. *Making a go of it* . . . what the hell is that? Seems to me that if you make enough of a *go* out of something it's probably a good idea to *leave*, or maybe even *stop* at some point, so let's just say I'm making a name for myself, which seems a whole lot less confusing. Also, it's way more useful than making a name for someone else.

I always tell people that I went to the greatest film school in the world, which prepared me for this career I am now making a go of. (Or, perhaps it should be *this career of which I am now making a go* . . . I'll make a go at getting back to you, but it's one or the other, I'm pretty sure, although I suppose you English-as-a-second-language types can make an argument for *this making a go of career*.) This line never fails to impress, although when it later comes up that I didn't bother to finish high school it begs a whole set of follow-up questions I'd prefer not to answer.

Here's the long-story-short version of why I stopped going to school: I wasn't that interested. Basically, it felt like a waste of my valuable time. At some point I figured out that whatever I *really* needed to learn I could read at the library. So that's what I did. I left the house for school each morning but went to the library instead. I didn't tell anybody—and, for the longest time, nobody noticed. That tells you what kind of impression I was making at school, I guess. It wasn't the most thoroughgoing institution. My teachers didn't know what to do with me. The other kids didn't know what to make of me. Even the school guidance counselor couldn't figure me out. She sat with me one day and tried to match my interests and talents to an appropriate career choice, and at the end of our meeting she threw up her hands and said, "Gilbert, I've got nothing. Good luck to you."

Then, just in case I missed her point, she said, "I can't even see you making money giving blood."

How's that for encouragement? I believe this woman took a special graduate school course in this type of guidance counseling, on how to handle underachieving Jews of no discernible intellect or aptitude. And I believe she paid careful attention in this special graduate school course, because the way she threw up her hands in exasperation was particularly effective. It told me in no uncertain terms that I wasn't cut out for this sort of thing—*this sort of thing* meaning an education, or a more traditional career path, or even a real job.

So I went to the library instead, and pursued my own independent course of study. I read a lot, back then. Books, magazines . . . whatever grabbed my interest. Usually it was books about monsters and magazines about monsters. Newspapers, I tended to avoid. Who had the time? Usually, there wouldn't be any stories about monsters, so I didn't see the point. Plus, as soon as you got through one edition, there was another to take its place and tell you everything it had gotten wrong the first time.

To this day, I avoid newspapers. There's quite a lot to read, and very often the ink comes off on your hands, especially when they run one of those big banner headlines on the front page. The bigger the news event, the bigger the mess. Like, when man first pretended to walk on the moon, on that soundstage in Houston. I was just a kid, so I didn't know enough to be jaded or above it all when it came to interpreting world events. I only knew that the front page of the newspaper was more dramatic-looking on some days than on others, so when I saw this big banner headline splashed across the front page of the *New York Post* I picked it up to see what all the fuss was about. Big mistake, it turned out. There was enough newsprint on that headline to make it look like my fingers had been dipped in coal. Then, a short while later, the newsprint rubbed off my own fingers and onto my dick, leaving Little Gilbert looking like something you might have found in Gary Coleman's pants—although, as far as I know, Gary Coleman hadn't even been born yet, so it would have been awkward for me to have been caught rummaging through his pants drawer like that. Probably, it would have been so awkward it would have made the news—with a big headline, which would have only led to more newsprint, more fingers looking like they had been dipped in coal, more postadolescent Jewish penises looking like they had been painted in blackface.

And so you see why I developed an aversion to newspapers. You read the paper, you get newsprint on your hands, the newsprint finds its way onto your dick, you fumble for ways to explain yourself in polite social company, you end up making the news yourself.

That kind of vicious cycle, I don't particularly need.

The reason I say I went to the greatest film school in the world is because we had a television, and I took full advantage. Now, you might read this and mumble to yourself, "Gilbert, what the hell are you talking about? Television in those days was nothing like television today. There were just a few channels. The reception was lousy. You're an idiot."

All of this was certainly true—but then, I'm not the idiot on the other side of the page, mumbling to myself as I flip through a minor work of nonfiction, so I must have learned *something* from watching all that television. At the very least, I learned not to talk back to a book. (Do this out in public— on a park bench, say—and people tend to move away from you, or start pointing.) But even more than that, I learned that sooner or later everything I needed to know about life and show business would filter through the rabbit ears on the black-and-white television set in our living room. It was like having a front-row seat to the whole wide world. And the best part: it came with catering. Most of the time, my mother would bring out a little tray of something for me to snack on as I watched and took notes. Other times, I could usually find enough crumbs in the cushions of the couch to keep from going hungry.

Back then, they'd always show these great old movies. They'd be edited for television, and sometimes there'd be huge chunks missing—like, the entire second act—but you'd get the idea. Boris Karloff, Danny Kaye, Greta Garbo, Buster Keaton . . . all these great stars, splashed across the small screen in our living room. Afternoons, I'd watch game shows, or *The 4:30 Movie* on Channel 7, the local ABC affiliate. Evenings, which we now know as "prime time" but was then known merely as "time," I watched variety shows and dramas and situation comedies. Sometimes, the only way I could tell the dramas from the situation comedies was because there were people laughing in the background on one type of program and not on the other. That was my cue—and despite the misgivings of my high school guidance counselor I was frequently able to make the distinction. Late at night, it was *The Tonight Show,* or some classic or not-so-classic horror film on *Chiller Theater* or *Creature Features.* All weekend long, it was one movie after another, sometimes grouped by theme. You could catch a Martin and Lewis marathon, or a Charlie Chan double bill, or a bunch of beach-blanket Gidget romps or Bowery Boys features. In fact, from the time of JFK's funeral to the time of RFK's funeral, I don't think we turned off the television set—except once or twice I might have pulled out the plug by accident, and another once or twice I might have warmed a cup of cocoa on top of the set and accidentally spilled some of it as I lifted the cup for a sip and had to shut it off while all those tubes dried out.

When it was working properly, and plugged in, there was an endless parade of news and entertainment coming through our television screen, in all shapes and sizes, and I took it all in. I wasn't exactly a discriminating viewer. If you put it on, and it was somewhat more interesting than what was showing on the other few channels, I'd sit back and watch. If I could jerk off to it, so much the better.

Oh, have I mentioned that I jerked off a lot? Do you even know whose book you're reading right now? When I was a kid, I would have jerked off to anything. When you're thirteen years old, you're just walking around with a twenty-four-hour hard-on. There's no such thing as *getting* a hard-on, and *maintaining* one isn't such an accomplishment, either. It's more like a constant state of being than a state of arousal. Some people might call it an affliction—and I was certainly well afflicted. I can still remember watching Bette Davis on *The Tonight Show,* when she was old and withered and paralyzed on one side of her face, but she was wearing a miniskirt and I could see a flash of skin. That was enough to get me going, and on a good night I could rub one out by the next commercial break.

Like the time I was staying up late to watch Claude Rains in *The Phantom of the Opera* on the small black-and-white television we had in our living room. My mother kept telling me to go to sleep, but I was determined to stay up and watch this movie on *The Late, Late, Late Show,* or whatever they called it at the time. Finally, my mother relented and brought me out a plate of crackers and butter and a glass of milk, which she placed on a folding TV table in front of me. Admittedly, I can no longer be sure after all these years that the night my mother brought me crackers and butter and a glass of milk coincided exactly with this late-night showing of *The Phantom of the Opera,* but it certainly happened from time to time. With or without the crackers and butter, it looked like a sweet, wholesome scene, until my mother went to bed and I turned on the television and they were still showing the last few minutes of the late local news. The final story on the news that night was about a girl who'd been attacked by a killer whale. It always surprises these people, a story like that. It's such a shocker. Who would have thought that something called a killer whale could actually kill people? And here, in black-and-white, was a grainy image of a girl just a few years older than me who had been riding on the back of the whale, wearing a bikini.

(Keep in mind, it was the girl wearing a bikini, not the whale, who probably didn't have the first idea where to shop for a bikini that didn't pinch him at the waist.)

I don't know how they captured this footage, back in the prehistoric, predigital camcorder era of my youth, but there was this pleasant-enough-looking girl, an employee at some warm-weather resort or marine park where they kept killer whales in swimming pools so tourists could climb on their backs and take home movies. And then for some inexplicable reason this particular whale went a little bit crazy and started chomping on this poor girl's leg. At least I think it was her leg. In any case, it was horrible.

There was a lot of commotion and the camerawork was lousy, but I could make out a couple guys jumping into the pool, trying to pull their co-worker from the whale's mouth. The girl finally got loose and someone other than the killer whale carried her to the side of the pool.

Now came the good part. Another couple guys started pulling this girl from the pool by her arms, and I could see that her bikini bottom had fallen to her knees in the struggle. That is, if she still had knees, at this point in the struggle. In any case, the bikini bottom was gone from the picture. Maybe the whale made off with it, thinking he might try it on later to see if it pinched at the waist. Or maybe he just realized he was a killer whale and he could pretty much do as he pleased. Nothing was left to my adolescent imagination. Nothing was pixilated or obscured in any way. Really, there was absolutely nothing to keep me from the crack of this girl's glorious ass, there for all of the New York metropolitan area to see.

It didn't matter to me just then that this girl's leg might have been missing, or that she was probably gushing blood. It didn't even occur to me to check for signs of life. It wouldn't have even registered if her head had been chomped off. All I could see was her killer body—and, once again, this was plenty. Still, I wanted more. (Just a little bit.) For a brief moment, I sat there hoping against hope that the rescue personnel would turn the girl around to face the camera, so I could see her pussy. I don't know if you've ever tried hoping against hope, but it's not an easy task, believe me. Hope itself is a mighty force, and when you push one mighty force against another, there's a good deal of resistance. If you're not careful, you might hurt yourself, and here I finally had to give up on the idea.

Still, it was an eyeful, and more than enough to get me going. As I recall, I had to race to my bed, to finish what the killer whale had inadvertently started, but I was quick enough about it that all I missed were the opening credits of *The Phantom of the Opera*. It helped that my bed was in the dining room, so I didn't have too far to go, and I made such quick work of myself that the opening credits were still scrolling when I got back to the television.

(There's probably a joke here, with a punch line that refers to the feel-good killer whale movie *Free Willy,* but I'm not about to make it. That would just be wrong.)

Somewhere in the middle of all that jerking off and watching television I learned a thing or two. I was a ready and eager pupil—*ready* and *eager* being two of my more persistent qualities. I paid attention. In fact, returning for a moment to my previous observation about talking back to the printed page, I seem to recall a scene in *The Ghost & Mrs. Muir*—the Hope Lange sitcom, not the Gene Tierney movie—where a character mumbled out loud to a book and was dismissed by the other characters as a nut, although I can't be certain. I never really paid attention to the show, so it's possible I was merely reading a little extra something into the scene. However, I didn't have be a fan or pay attention to find something to jerk off to in the sitcom *and* the movie, because Hope Lange and Gene Tierney were both pretty easy on the eyes, as we say in the self-love business—something else I learned from watching all that television.

Another thing I learned from *The Ghost & Mrs. Muir*: Charles Nelson Reilly actually had a *career*, before becoming a staple of afternoon game shows and dinner theater revivals of Rodgers & Hammerstein musicals that featured sexually ambiguous supporting characters. Of course, this was a time when flaming homosexuals in movies and on television were never looked upon as gay so much as eccentric. Now, when you watch Paul Lynde sing in *Bye Bye Birdie* about what's the matter with kids these days, you can't help but think, *Gee, I don't know, Paul. It takes more than one chocolate bar to get them into your van?*

Soon, I came to the conclusion that I was destined for a career of my own in show business. Well, strike that. Maybe *destined* is too strong a word in this context, because it suggests something epic or biblical or otherwise significant, and far be it from me to confuse myself with anything epic or biblical or otherwise significant. And as long as I'm striking *destined*, I might as well do away with *career* as well, because it suggests something . . . well, a little more remarkable than the bookings and gigs I've managed to string together over the years. So as long as destiny wasn't part of the equation, and since a more traditional career path seemed out of the question, show business seemed like a good place to hide. In show business, at least, I could get away with being a little odd or idiosyncratic or ill-suited for polite social company. In the rest of the world, if you were stupid or neurotic or a fucked-up pain in the ass, people tended to notice, but these qualities were held up and admired in show business. Here's an example: Marlon Brando could be a complete screwball, in every possible way, and people would only talk about his genius. Some interviewer would ask him how he prepared for a part, and he'd say he thinks about a green bagel, and all over the country aspiring actors would start thinking about green bagels as if this was the key to success. Really, that man was the best thing to happen to the green bagel business since St. Patrick's Day happened to fall just after Passover.

A career in show business was like a free pass. It meant you could get away with anything—or, it was my fervent hope, without doing much of anything at all. So that was settled. I wouldn't bother going to school. I'd go to the library and watch a lot of television instead. In this way, I supposed, I'd stumble into show business. I'd find a side door and slip my way inside. All that was left was for me to figure out what the hell I would actually do to earn myself this free pass. I couldn't sing. I couldn't dance. I wasn't particularly good-looking. Like I said, I had no discernible talent or admirable qualities, although I did like to do voices. I don't think I was particularly good at doing voices, but I enjoyed myself just the same. Eventually, it got to where I could imitate people off of television and do a decent enough job of it that my two older sisters could figure out who I was imitating. To me, this was a great victory. I mean, that's the whole point, isn't it? You *do* Henny Youngman, the people on the receiving end of your performance should at least recognize that the person you're *doing* is supposed to be Henny Youngman.

That's pretty much the bare-minimum standard, and I rose to meet it. Like here: a man says to a pretty waitress, "You look tired. Why don't you go up to my room and lie down?" It's a funny line, right, but it's only a little bit funny until you say it like Henny Youngman. Then, it's a whole lot funnier.

Once, not too long after I'd started working as a comic, I had the chance to meet Henny Youngman. (I'm getting ahead of the story, I know, but you look like you're in good shape. You can catch up.) We had the same agent, and he arranged it. At least he was good for something. We met out in front of the agent's office. I could see Henny walking toward me from halfway down the street, carrying his violin case. When he reached me, I put out my hand, thinking we would shake hands, but he just handed me his violin case. He said, "Are you married?"

I told him I wasn't.

He said, "So what do you do for aggravation?"

But that came later. First I had to find that side door and sneak into show business. For that, I needed a small push. One day, my sister Arlene told one of her friends about my emerging talent for doing voices. All these years later, it's unclear to me if she was bragging about her little brother, or apologizing for my odd behavior, but in any case it turned out her friend had an idea. He told her about the Bitter End, a club in Greenwich Village where they had something called Hootenanny Night. This was back before the stand-up comedy boom of the 1970s, when all these different comedy clubs started opening up around the city. Hootenanny Night was mostly like amateur night at the Apollo Theatre, only instead of a bunch of black people trying to sound like James Brown or Little Stevie Wonder you had a bunch of entitled Jews trying to sound like Bob Dylan or Pete Seeger.

Arlene and my other sister, Karen, agreed that Hootenanny Night at the Bitter End would be a good venue for my emerging talents, which by this point had emerged all over our apartment and were looking for a bigger room. So they came to me one day and suggested I perform at the Bitter End. It's possible they suggested this in unison—as in, "Gilbert, we think you should perform at the Bitter End," like they'd put it to a vote—although I can't recall. Whenever I ask them about this now, neither one of them will take the credit for me becoming a comedian, which they very sweetly refer to as *accepting blame*, which is almost like the same thing. Still, there's no disputing that they came to me one day and offered to take me to Greenwich Village.

I was fifteen years old, and the reason my sisters offered to take me was because I hadn't figured out how to ride the subways by myself. I didn't really need their moral support. I wasn't smart enough to feel stage fright or performance jitters. I just needed them to hold my hand and take me on the subway—basically, to make sure I didn't get lost. The deal was, if I didn't bomb, they would also take me home.

I didn't know enough to check things out beforehand. If I'd thought about it at all, I might have gone to a couple of Hootenanny Nights before stepping out on that stage, just to get some idea what I was getting myself into, but I wasn't the type to think things through. It didn't even occur to me to prepare any material. I just went backstage and gave the emcee my name and waited to be called. I think I followed a guy doing Arlo Guthrie. Or maybe it was a guy doing Joan Baez. When my turn came, I stepped to the microphone and started talking. I did Groucho Marx. In those days, I did the young Groucho. Since then, I've become famous for my old Groucho, but my act had yet to mature. I also did Peter Lorre and Bela Lugosi, which meant that even in 1969 my act was a bit dated. Even in 1949, my act would have been a bit dated, but who am I to quibble?

I wish I could remember my first few jokes. And I wish I could remember if people laughed. Nobody booed or threw anything, though, so I guess it went well enough. Plus, my sisters ended up taking me home—another strong indicator. They didn't tell me I sucked or that I should probably rethink this not-going-to-school business, so I vowed to go back to the Bitter End the following week, for the next Hootenanny Night.

And the one after that. And the one after that.

Before long, I was a Hootenannying fool. (If you asked my father, he would have told you I was just a regular fool, but far be it from me to keep from turning a fun-filled word like *Hootenanny* into a descriptive phrase.) I still didn't have an act, and it would be years before I had the good sense to prepare any material. At some point, after years and years of performing onstage, I developed a routine. Each time out, my impressions would be a little less lame, a little less bottom-of-the-barrel. Gradually, I moved from doing impressions to telling jokes. And, also gradually, I brought my material more and more up to date. By 1979, I was doing some killer Woodstock material. By 1999, I'd retired my peanut farmer jokes for bits about the Gipper and *Bedtime for Bonzo*. By 2009, I'd finally gotten around to Monica Lewinsky.

Some nights, I killed. Other nights, not so much . . . I started hanging out with other comics, working at other clubs, working on my act. In fact, it wasn't until this time that I even thought of what I was doing as an *act*. I was just telling jokes, doing impressions, trying to make people laugh. One night I met another comic who brought a tape recorder to his shows, so he could listen to his performance and make some refinements, and that seemed like a good idea. However, it also seemed like too much trouble, so I didn't bother.

I worked the New York comedy circuit before it could even be called a circuit. It was more like an unmarked trail. Most of the time, I'd go to some club and wait around until three o'clock in the morning before it even occurred to anyone that I hadn't gotten on. More often than not, I'd wind up at Catch, which was what those of us in the know called Catch a Rising Star, which had quickly become *the* place for young comics to work on new material and hope like hell to get noticed by some talent agent looking to cast a forgettable sitcom—or, at least, that's what the club owner told us to keep us working for free. There were a couple times at Catch when the emcee would be onstage, looking out across the club, desperate for another comic to step up to the microphone. There'd be like an hour to go before closing, and he'd be looking right at me and saying, "Jesus, folks, this has never happened before. We've run out of comics."

This was not a good sign, as far as my fledgling career or my flagging self-esteem were concerned, but fortunately for me and my tens of fans I was never any good at picking up on stuff like this. For example, I never thought it was unusual that I didn't get paid on those nights when I actually did get to go on, because none of the comics I knew got paid for performing. It wasn't really part of the deal. Once, a bartender took pity on me at some club, when he saw me waiting half the night to go on, and he came over with a glass of Coke, which I counted as my first piece of compensation. I arrived home that night just as my mother was getting up to start her day, and I very proudly told her of my first rush of success. "I got a free glass of Coke tonight," I said, my chest bursting.

It was hard to tell, but I believe the look I got back in return was one of enormous shared pride. After all, I was now one step closer to being able to support myself. So, yeah, I'm pretty sure that's what it was, enormous shared pride. That, or it was something she ate.

Another time, I was at the Comic Strip, where the emcee was also known to look right past me when he needed another few sets to close out the night. I was working with a comic who shall remain nameless in these pages—mostly because his career never amounted to anything and he did remain nameless. If I told you his name, you'd have no idea who I was talking about, even though it would amuse me and a few other comics who also worked with this guy. On this particular night, this particular comic got lucky and hooked up with a girl from the audience. This happened sometimes, I was told, although it never happened to me. Whenever a girl from the audience tried to throw herself at me, she'd turn out to have terrible aim. She'd wind up fifty miles away.

This girl from the audience hung around until closing time, at which point she and this unknown comic started messing around onstage. (Talk about losing your audience!) While he was fucking her, the lucky comic was going at it with such wild abandon that his colostomy bag burst open.

He told us the story the next night like it was the funniest thing in the world, but no matter how he dressed it up it came out sounding like one of those *I-guess-you-had-to-be-there* stories. If I *had* been there, two things would have likely happened. One, I would have stood in the wings with my digital camcorder and invented YouTube right there on the spot, because a thing like this, it should be shared with the entire universe. And two, I would have finally gotten lucky myself, or so I like to think, because all of a sudden I would have looked pretty damn good, standing next to a guy like this. I would have turned to this girl from the audience and said, "Hey, at least I won't shit on you."

I still remember the first time I got paid for telling jokes, which in the end turned out to be a far more likely scenario than me getting laid for telling jokes. It was in the basement of some church. I could do no wrong that night, as I recall. I was on comedy fire. I was hot, hot, hot. In stand-up circles, we comedians have a phrase we like to use to describe one of those nights when we're especially on, when everything seems to work and the audience catches every piece of cleverness and nuance in our material. It's called *one of those nights when we're especially on, when everything seems to work and the audience catches every piece of cleverness and nuance in our material.*

I was like the Beatles at Shea Stadium, only you could actually hear what I was saying and I didn't get laid afterward. All I got was seven dollars, which seemed to me like all the money in the world.

I went back to that church a couple weeks later, when my seven dollars ran out, hoping for more of the same, only this time I bombed. This time, I was like the Mets at Shea Stadium—which, I'll confess, is not a line that's original to me. You see, I don't know anything about baseball, so I bought that line from a guy at a comedy club who seemed to need the money. To be accurate, I didn't actually *buy* the line from this guy, but I did give him half of my sandwich. (Okay, okay . . . if you really want to know the truth, I let him have two bites.)

Just to clarify, I don't know or care a thing about sports, except I seem to recall hearing that Babe Ruth was fat—which now that I think about it makes a whole lot of sense because he must have eaten a lot of his candy bars.

(Gee, maybe I've been fooling myself, all this time. Maybe I know a lot more about baseball than I let on.)

Some of my first gigs were so far off on the fringes of show business you could hardly recognize the neighborhood. Once, I worked at a synagogue event with a conservatively dressed lounge singer named Pat Benatar. She sang that song from *Godspell,* the Jesus Christ musical, the one about finding her corner of the sky. I always hated that song, because there are just too many people in this world and not enough corners to go around, but she sang it well enough. You could almost dance to it—or, at least, not puke to it. Still, I didn't think she'd go very far in show business, because by this point I was a wise old veteran of show business and a shrewd judge of talent.

Another time, I went out on a booking to an address I didn't recognize and when I got there I saw that it wasn't a club or a bar. It wasn't even a church or a synagogue or a public meeting place of any kind. It was just an apartment building, which I thought was strange. But what the hell did I care? A gig was a gig. Money was money. So I rode the elevator to this giant, decrepit loft. It was dark and dreary and mostly empty. There were four or five folding chairs, and a few tables set about the room. On the tables were a bunch of pamphlets or flyers—from the looks of things, they could have been left over from an Eisenhower rally.

A creepy-looking guy stepped out of the darkness to greet me. He said, "No blue material, kid. You go on at eight-fifteen."

It was about eight o'clock already, and it was just me and him. It was the same guy who hired me, a couple nights earlier, backstage at one of the comedy clubs, only in that setting he didn't look so creepy. I thought, *This can't be good.* So I made some excuse. I said, "Do I have time to step outside for a smoke, before I go on?"

The creepy-looking guy said, "Sure, kid. But remember, no blue material."

I nodded—then I raced downstairs and never came back.

I'd go anywhere for a gig when I was just starting out, even all the way to Canada. One of my very first shows outside New York was in a run-down club in Ottawa. It was during a ridiculous cold spell, which was even cold by Canadian standards. It was like a million degrees below zero—and that's not even counting the exchange rate. There was no way to keep warm, and I was supposed to do three twenty-minute shows, back-to-back-to-back. There was no opening act, no emcee, no stage. There was a microphone set up in a corner of the bar area, at the same level as the cold, drunken Canadian patrons, but there was no way to tell if it even worked. Before my first show, a woman who could barely speak English stood on the other side of the room and introduced me. She just yelled my name out, and the people at the bar stopped talking for a moment.

Surprisingly, some people showed up for my very first show, although it's possible they had just stepped inside to get warm. It was just horrible. No one knew who I was—although this alone wasn't so unusual, because even in New York no one knew who I was. I told a few jokes. No one laughed. It's possible the microphone wasn't working and they couldn't hear me, but I kept going for twenty minutes.

Then I stepped away from the microphone, to stunned

silence, occasionally broken by shouts of "You suck!" I thought I heard some applause, but then I realized the people were just trying to keep their hands warm, clapping them together like that.

A short while later, I started on another twenty-minute set—*to the same roomful of people!* I couldn't believe it. I didn't think I'd have enough material to get me through a third set, so I started improvising. I got it in my head that I didn't give a shit, which I learned was a great approach. I went a little crazy, and soon enough the audience was going a little crazy right along with me. The microphone was working, after all. The cold Canadians were warming up. They were laughing and clapping each other on the back and buying each other drinks and having a grand old time. Before I knew it, I looked up and saw that I'd been performing for about an hour and a half, so I stepped away from the microphone again—this time to somewhat more meaningful applause.

Then, after another short break, I went back on and did fifteen minutes, thinking since I'd gone way over on that second set I was in good shape. I did another few jokes, and another few impressions, and thought I'd call it a night, only when the owner of the club came up to me afterward he didn't look too happy.

He said, "You owe me five minutes."

And then, to top off the experience, I got home and discovered that his check bounced.

It was always a moment of great significance, back when I first started working in clubs, when a comic made it to the *Tonight Show* stage for the first time. It was like graduating one of our own. At every comedy club in the country, a television behind the bar would be tuned to Johnny Carson, and time would stand still for three or four minutes while the comedian performed. Even the waitresses would watch, and they'd jump up and down like they were receiving some secret message from the comedy gods—which, in a way, they were. Among stand-up comedians, this was the closest we'd come to a holy, religious moment.

I never really bought into the whole Carson mystique, so I would always stand back at some remove from the scene, as the other comics read all these signs into what we were watching. If Johnny would play with his tie a certain way or tap his pencil on his desk a certain number of times, it was said to mean one thing. If he asked the comic to cross from his spot at center stage and join him on the couch, it meant that the skies had opened up and the heavens had parted and he was bestowing stardom upon this unknown person.

Like idiots, or sheep, or quite possibly an entire flock of really stupid sheep, we convinced ourselves that if you did a good set on Carson you'd have a career, although in reality there were just a handful of performers who became stars after one successful *Tonight Show* appearance. It didn't hurt, killing on *The Tonight Show,* but it wasn't exactly a Golden Ticket to a long, name-above-the-title career, either. If you don't believe me, just Google Daphne Davis—an Australian comic who was briefly in Carson's favor, until she wasn't, after which she changed her name to Maureen Murphy and tried to fool us into thinking she was an undiscovered talent. Me, I wasn't quite there yet—and I wouldn't be for some time. I had a lot of shit jobs to slog through before appearing on network television.

I had another memorably crappy gig in Texas, early on in my career. This one was in a club that looked like it had been built with Scotch tape and cardboard. As the son of a hardware store owner, I knew a thing or two about construction, and I could tell this building was poorly constructed. This alone wasn't saying much. Even if I was the son of a baker, it would have looked pretty bad. Really, the place was like a thrown-together shack. The offices and dressing rooms backstage looked like they had been built from the cheapest plywood, nailed to wooden poles. If you sneezed too hard, the walls would have come down. Plus, the walls didn't even reach all the way to the ceiling.

So there I was, minding my own business backstage, marveling at the shabby construction, when I happened to notice two Mexicans climbing up into the crawl space between the top of the walls and the actual ceiling. I thought this was a curious thing and wondered what they were doing. I guess the Mexicans could tell that I was looking at them, and wondering this very thing, because they smiled at me in Spanish and suggested I join them.

Me being quite stupid, I said, "Okay," which they didn't understand. Then we all looked at each other in a confused sort of way for a while, until one of the Mexicans approached and helped to hoist me up to the crawl space, which the weight of a roach might have collapsed. Then we started crawling. With one wetback in front of me, and another behind me, we crawled like rats on these flimsy wooden beams. It felt to me like our crawling was causing all the rooms to shake like we were in the middle of a giant earthquake.

Then we came to a stop. The Mexican in front looked

back at me, his non-English-speaking smile wider than ever. He gestured toward some big pieces of cardboard, which had been laid out on the floor of the crawl space, covering the wooden beams. He seemed to want me to stretch out and relax on one of these big pieces of cardboard, so like an idiot I did just that, and as I did I could see that several holes had been poked into the cardboard every here and there. Then the Mexican who had been behind me seemed to indicate that I should look through one of these holes, very excitedly.

And so, of course, I did. I had come this far, and these particular wetbacks must have seemed like very trustworthy fellows. So I looked through one of the holes—right down into the ladies' room. It was like a scene out of a Mexican remake of *Porky's,* and I treated myself to the sight of women relieving themselves on the toilets below. It was quite an eyeful. As I looked, my new Mexican friends started slapping me on the back, quite pleased with themselves. I still didn't understand a word of what they were saying, but their smiles had grown even wider.

After three hours of this, I realized that what they were doing was tasteless and immature. Not only that, I started to worry that the entire structure was about to collapse into dust, and I would fall to my death, crushing some poor woman trying to take a dump. The thought was just too much for me at that time. And by *too much* I mean too much of a turn-on, although now that I think about it, if I had my choice, it's not such a bad way to go. Plus, it would have been a good career move.

You'll be happy to know that this very same club discriminated against men, in something like the same way. Also, it

turned out to be Ground Zero for a stock line used by comedy club emcees all across this great land. You know how
there are generic lines or jokes you hear over and over? You
hear them so often, no one knows who came up with them
in the first place. Well, at this particular club, when the emcee saw a girl stand up in the middle of a set to go to the ladies' room, the emcee would say, "Oh, you're going to the
ladies' room. Let's turn on the hidden microphone." Only
here it wasn't a joke. There actually was a hidden microphone
in the ladies' room, so you could listen to all these lovely
cowgirls grunt and fart and empty their bladders in epic ways.

Personally, I didn't see the appeal. The peepholes through
the cardboard ceiling looking down, I could certainly understand. Those had some redeeming social value. But hidden
microphones? Some things were better left to the imagination.

At one point, I had to go to the bathroom, and I asked
someone who worked there, "They don't have a hidden mike
in the men's room, do they?"

He said, "No. Just the ladies' room."

I asked, "Why don't they have one in the men's room, too?"

He said, "Because our male customers carry guns and
they'll shoot you if they catch you listening."

Over the years, in between all of these odd, crappy comedy gigs, I worked at a bunch of odd, crappy regular-person
jobs, to subsidize my stand-up habit. Do I really need to tell
you these were odd, crappy jobs? It's not like you're thinking,
after I stopped going to high school, that I somehow landed a
job as a neurosurgeon but it just didn't work out. I worked for
a while as a messenger, until someone pointed out to me that

I would have an easier time pedaling around town and making my deliveries without training wheels. For another while, I worked on a kind of assembly line at a factory that made antiburglary kits. It was an unusual product that somehow let those of us involved in the making of it delude ourselves into thinking we were working for the public good. One of the items in the kit was a tiny metal pencil that was meant to be used to scrape or scratch a special marking into your valuables so you could recover them if they were stolen. I sat at a table with a big carton of these metal pencils and a glass ashtray, and worked my way through the carton to see which pencils cut easily through the glass. The ones that worked, I put into the *good* pile. The ones that didn't work, I put into the *bad* pile. After all the products were tested, we slapped a label on the kit that said "Tested by Skilled Craftsmen." For years, I took girls up and down the aisles of stores that sold these kits and pointed to the label and said, "You see that, where it says 'Skilled Craftsmen'? That's me."

It was a professional highlight, although I must confess that the kits seemed to prevent more than just burglaries. They also prevented me from getting laid or impressing any women.

The closest I came to landing an actual show business job was working the concession stands in Broadway theaters, selling T-shirts and drinks and overpriced candy. I got the job through another comic, who also needed to support his stand-up habit. The way it worked was that one guy owned the concessions in a bunch of different theaters, and we struggling comics or out-of-work actors would move from theater to theater, wherever we were needed. There were a lot of great shows playing on Broadway at the time, so I got another fine education. It was like taking an extension course, after watching all that television. There was *American Buffalo,* with Robert Duvall and John Savage. There was *Equus,* with Richard Burton. For a while, Richard Burton had to take a temporary leave, which I believe was what he did of his senses every time he married Elizabeth Taylor, and he was replaced by Anthony Perkins.

The best part about working the concessions at *Equus* was the show's famous nude scene. After I sat through the show a time or two, I had it all timed out. I'd go downstairs and relax in the lobby and listen for a certain speech, which was my signal to hurry back to my post in time to watch this girl take her clothes off onstage. This was another career highlight—for me, not the girl. My only regret was that I couldn't jerk off to it. There were too many people around, and the couple times I tried I came all over the overpriced candy, which I was told was bad for business.

(Who knew?)

For another stretch, I worked the concession at a show called A *Matter of Gravity,* with Katharine Hepburn. This, too, was a career highlight—once again, for me. Katharine Hepburn was one of the few Broadway stars who took the time to talk to us lowly concession workers. The routine was we'd have to get to the theater before the doors opened, and she would be there early before heading to her dressing room to get into costume, and a lot of times we'd all hang out in the lobby or at the foot of the stage, swapping stories, although by *swapping* I really mean listening to Katharine Hepburn's stories. I can't imagine she would have been all that interested in hearing about the time I came all over the overpriced candy at *Equus* or the time my buddy shit all over that girl from the audience while he was fucking her—and, tellingly, I knew enough not to bring up such matters of gravity.

Katharine Hepburn's big thing was to keep the theater properly ventilated. She hated that it was so stuffy inside that old theater, and insisted that we fling open the doors as soon as we arrived. We were all very much in awe of the great Katharine Hepburn, so we did just that. We were all so damn eager to please. Whichever one of us got to the theater first would make sure to open the doors and air the place out. She seemed to appreciate it.

Some days, I'd find myself heading to the theater a couple hours before curtain time, just for the chance to hang out with my new pal Kate, and shoot the shit about our mutual acquaintances, Cagney and Bogart and Tracy. She'd talk about them as intimates (and here it helps if you imagine me doing a pitch-perfect Katharine Hepburn impression): "Jimmy and Bogie and Spence."

(It also helps if you add the lilt and quiver to Hepburn's late-in-life voice, although it's tough to bring across Parkinson's on the page—at least it's tough to do so with anything resembling good taste. Try this: hold the book a few inches out in front of you as you read, and then start shaking it like a rattle. Very briskly. Or, if you're listening to me in an audio format, turn the volume up and down, and play with the pause button. That should do it.)

James Cagney had just published his autobiography, and one day Hepburn came in and gushed, "Oh, you simply must read Jimmy's book. It's a wonderful book, Jimmy's book. It's just marvelous, Jimmy's book. It's so inspiring, Jimmy's book."

And on and on . . .

A few days later, Kate was in a foul mood because we'd apparently forgotten to open the doors. She was a tough old bird, even then, and she flashed us looks that made us feel like morons. There's no denying that we were, in fact, morons, but we didn't appreciate being made to feel that way by such a legend of stage and screen. Then the great Katharine Hepburn stormed about the theater in a huff, making a big show of throwing open the doors herself, in such a way as to give off the impression that it was so very difficult to get good help these days.

The next day, she came in early and called us all onto the stage. The theater was empty. This time, we'd all made certain that the doors had been flung open. We couldn't imagine why we had been summoned. When we got to the stage, we saw that she was carrying a big pile of books—Cagney's book, it turned out. She gave each of us a copy, which she of course signed. It struck me as the most generous, heartfelt gesture, which is why I felt like such a shit when I took it down to the Strand later that week and traded it in for a couple bucks. And get this: the guy at the Strand said he would have given me a couple bucks more if the book had actually been signed by the author, instead of by a tough old bird like Katharine Hepburn, so I felt bad about that, too. I mean, how hard would it have been for Kate to have asked her precious Jimmy to scrawl his name on a couple extra copies of his book?

And so if you went to see *Equus* or *American Buffalo* or *A Matter of Gravity* during the middle 1970s, there's a good chance you're familiar with my early work in the theater. There's also a good chance that if you were kind enough to tip the guy behind the concession stand or the coat-check guy the money never made it into my hands, because the jerk who owned the concession kept all the tips for himself. We got back at him by doubling the price of his drinks and pocketing the difference— which, after all, we certainly felt entitled to. I mention this in case any of you want to try again and forward the money to me through my publisher. After all, if you were satisfied with my work and wanted to show your appreciation, I'd hate to cheat you out of the opportunity.

Clip 'n' Save Joke no. 5 ✂

A woman is on her hospital deathbed. Her hair is all dried out. Her skin is extremely pale. Her breathing is labored. Her eyes are completely clouded over. Her husband is grieving, sitting quietly at the corner of the bed. They sit together for a while, until finally the woman wheezes out one final request. "Please, honey," she says, "could you fuck me in the ass?"

At first, the husband isn't sure he's heard his wife correctly. She senses his confusion and repeats the request. "Could you fuck me in the ass?" she says again.

The husband is surprised by his wife's request, but he looks around the room and figures he can certainly do this one small thing for her. It's the least he can do, he tells himself.

He closes the curtains for privacy and climbs on the bed. As he's fucking her in the ass, his wife's shallow breath becomes deeper and deeper. Then she starts moaning louder and louder. After that, she starts screaming with pleasure. All of a sudden, her hair begins to look vibrant and full. The color returns to her skin. She jumps from the bed looking healthier and sexier than she has in years.

Seeing this, the husband begins to cry. He sits on the corner of the bed and starts bawling like a baby.

"Please, honey," his wife says. "Don't cry. What could be wrong?"

The husband has had his face buried in his hands, but he now looks up to his wife, tears streaming down his cheeks, and says, "I could have saved my father!"

5

My Brilliant Career

I must apologize for this chapter title, because it doesn't accurately reflect my assessment of my life's work. Don't misunderstand, I enjoy my work as much as the next person (okay, maybe just a little bit more), but I'm not one of those Hollywood types who is so full of himself he tosses around words like *brilliant* or *luminous* or *astounding* to describe his talents, at least not in public. Actually, *luminous* isn't half-bad, and I think I'll start working it into conversations about me (which, to be clear, are some of my very favorite conversations) because it can refer to my many and varied gifts as an actor and comedian, as well as to the supple softness of my even-toned, healthy-looking skin.

Let me just finish up about this chapter title, because I don't feel great about it. Believe me, if there was a hardly seen Australian movie called *My Mediocre Career* or *My at One Time Promising But Ultimately Disappointing Career*, I would have almost certainly used that instead. But I'm stuck with brilliance, I guess. It's the story of my life, really. It's like I stepped in shit and it's been following me around on my shoe. I just can't get rid of it. *Brilliant, brilliant, brilliant.* For years now, it's all I've been hearing—and, frankly, I've had it up to here with all this talk of my sheer comic genius.

"Up to where?" you might say.

My point exactly.

And so, my career . . .

I bounced around those New York comedy clubs for years and years. Occasionally, I climbed onstage and told jokes. Most of the time, people waited politely for me to finish my act and didn't bother saying anything to me afterward. Even my fellow comedians tended to ignore me, unless it was to share a story of fucking and shitting on some after-hours stage. However, a few people made the mistake of telling me I was funny, and like a fool I chose to believe them. Unfortunately, the people who told me this didn't happen to be seated in the comedy clubs in and around New York where I tended to perform, so I had to content myself early on with mostly smiles of recognition from audiences that would have probably preferred the comedy stylings of some other young comedian. And yet, over time people started to laugh, against their better judgment. I could only assume they were laughing at my jokes, and not at me directly, but I was not about to question their laughter. It was enough that I was working in bigger clubs, in better time slots, when people were actually eager to be entertained instead of kept awake.

Despite my best efforts, I looked up one day, one month, one year and realized I was having some small success on the comedy club circuit, which was about what I deserved. You know how it is: one small success leads to another, until you've strung together all these small successes and you've got nothing to show for it. That was me, until some people from MTV happened to see my act one night at Catch. Probably they were waiting for their waitress to bring them their drinks and they'd run out of things to talk about with each other, so they turned their attention to the annoying little man on stage. And it's a good thing they did. They were looking for a way to kill time between music videos, it turned out. Now it's gotten to where you'd have to be a detective to even find a music video on MTV, but in the early 1980s this was a revolutionary idea for them. They were producing a series of long-form, in-house commercials, which were really just brief comedy bits or stand-alone sketches. The MTV people had no idea what they were doing, really, which worked out well for me because neither did I. Happily, we found each other, and I ended up doing a bunch of these "in-between" segments for them. We did them all in one afternoon. Everything was ad-libbed, except for the part where we mentioned MTV. That part was libbed. At first, our agreement was that I would do all of this ad-libbing for free, in exchange for the exposure and some cheese and crackers, but as the day dragged on I started to whine a little bit. The MTV people didn't know if this was just my annoying personality or some pathetic eleventh-hour negotiating strategy, meant to extort huge sums from their corporate accounts. Either way, the whining was effective, because they ended up paying me $500 for a day of work, which at the time was more money than I'd ever earned for one gig. (And this was before taking all that cheese and crackers into account.)

I was so excited about my big payday, I had to tell someone. Like an idiot, I told my agent, who shared my enthusiasm long enough to say, "That's great, Gilbert. How would you like to handle our commission?"

I continued to work with this agent for many years. I kept meaning to fire her, but I didn't know how. Finally, the agency fired her, so I didn't have to. She never really *got* me, this agent. I don't wish to give her name, but for the book let's just call her Asshole. Here's what I mean when I say she didn't get me: when MTV started airing these spots, I kept hearing from everybody how funny and brilliant I was. That is, I heard this from everybody except this Asshole (not her real name). She kept telling me and anyone else who called to see about booking me that the reason the spots worked so well was because MTV must have hired a brilliant director. There was no other way to explain it, she said, because my act had never worked on television before.

Looking back, I think my asshole agent thought of me as Rin Tin Tin—or, Lassie, if you prefer a more contemporary reference.

One more thing about my asshole agent. She was soon replaced by another asshole agent. This one was a real go-getter. He'd seen my act and thought I was great, a real up-and-comer. (And, for those of you unfamiliar with the entertainment industry, when you combine a real go-getter with a real up-and-comer, it's neither here nor there.) He went to his colleagues and said, "I just saw this comedian, Gilbert Gottfried. Does anybody know who handles him?" Nobody knew, so they looked it up and said, "Oh, he's signed with us."

I didn't have anything better to do so I started working

with this guy. For purposes of the book, and to avoid the possibility of any legal action, let's just call him my new-and-improved asshole agent. He was a real Hollywood type. He pushed me to sign with a manager, a public relations company, the whole deal. I was busy, busy, busy. They had me running all over town, taking meetings, reading scripts. I had everything a movie star should have, with the exception of work, money, fame and women. Other than that, I had it covered.

MTV started showing the crap out of those things, and people began to notice me. One thing led to another—which it has a tendency to do, I'm told—and before long these one and another things were starting to look like a career. Or, something resembling a career. Bill Cosby called, looking for "that abrasive comic who's always on MTV." He wanted me to audition for a guest spot on *The Cosby Show*. It was the number one show on television, so my first reaction was that there had been some horrible mistake. When my asshole agent called with the opportunity, I thought maybe I was auditioning to be Cosby's long-lost cousin, but they had something else in mind.

I later learned that the producers originally wanted me to be one of the Cosbys, but when they screen-tested me I looked too black.

My bad, homie. (Oh, and as another of my many literary innovations, please note this parenthetical stage direction: I'm punching my fist against my chest as I write this, and sticking out two fingers, and embracing my loyal readers with a figurative soul handshake and hug.)

Here, I'd like to put my story on pause for a moment and share a show business observation.

Early on in my career, I discovered the three biggest lies in Hollywood. In no particular order, they are:

1. *The check's in the mail.*
2. *We can fix it in editing.*
3. *Gilbert Gottfried gets a lot of pussy.*

Okay, now let's get back to our regularly scheduled story . . .

Things were mostly hit-or-miss for me, when I was just starting out, only my "hits" seemed to take the form of angry comedy club patrons who wanted to slap me around because they didn't think I was particularly funny, and my "misses" were so wide of the mark you could hardly notice I was even there. I went out on a lot of auditions, as I recall. I even auditioned for a part opposite a talking orangutan, which came as something of a surprise to me because I'd always thought orangutan was spelled *orangutang*. (Apparently, I'd confused the species with a wildly unpopular simian space drink.) Also, I wasn't aware that orangutans could talk, but here again I was wrong. The part was for a pilot being developed by Barry Levinson, before he became known for being from Baltimore instead of working with apes. I actually got the job, although I've always suspected that Mr. Levinson might have mistaken me for one of the orangutans, because I hadn't waxed my back that week and I'd been carrying some excess winter weight at the time of the audition.

Surprisingly, the show wasn't picked up by the network, but I did get some valuable experience out of the deal. I also developed some important contacts, because as we all know

Hollywood is a town built on relationships, even though in this case those relationships were with a bunch of orangutans.

A short time later, those key professional relationships came back into play when I went out on another audition for a show with orangutans. (Apparently, orangutans were well represented back then, because those fuckers were *everywhere*.) This show was a sitcom called *Mr. Smith*, and as far as I could tell it was about an orangutan that wore a suit and worked as a corporate executive. This was what used to be known in television as a high-concept, because the writers who thought it up were high out of their minds.

Here's a little bit more than you need to know about this low moment in television history: the role of Mr. Smith was played by three different orangutans, which the producers would shuttle on and off the set according to the animals' moods—or, perhaps, to their particular emotive strengths, depending on the scene. There was also an animatronic monkey that would be wheeled in from time to time, for certain shots, only it was the most terrifying animatronic monkey anybody had ever seen. Even in the auditions, I could see that it didn't work very well. It had dead, waxy eyes, and the mouth never quite moved in sync with the voice, and the hands couldn't grab or grip the way they were supposed to. Basically, it looked like something that would frighten a small child, especially if that child happened to be a member of a Nielsen family, which perhaps explains why the show never caught on.

As it turned out, the "lead" orangutan was one of the same damn orangutans from the Barry Levinson pilot that went nowhere. When I first made the connection, I thought it could only mean that I would certainly get the part. After all, we'd gotten along so well. We'd had some laughs, and seemed to enjoy each other's company, but apparently I'd rubbed this damn ape the wrong way. (And here I'd been thinking that all those moans and sighs and ape ejaculate were a good thing.) I know this because the animal seemed to remember me and sidled over to the producers' table while I read my lines and announced that he refused to work with me.

In the end, I didn't get the part, but *Mr. Smith* did send over a nice note and promised to call me.

Other actors and comedians, their careers seem to move on a kind of upward trajectory. Me, I just grabbed whatever I could, in my hit-or-miss way, and hoped for the best. The one thing I had going for me, people always said, was that I was funny. I've said this already, I know, but I'm of the opinion that you can never say enough nice things about yourself, and that some of these nice things are worth repeating. I suppose it's possible that some of these people might have meant that I was *funny-looking* or *funny-sounding*. It's possible, too, that I might have given off a funny smell, but what the hell did I care? Funny was funny.

Eventually, *funny* took me all the way to the *Saturday Night Live* audition I wrote about earlier. I probably should have looked at this as my big break, but I didn't know enough to be nervous. I just went in and told a few jokes and did a few voices and hoped the people would like me well enough to call me back.

It was quite a scene at the audition. There were no orangutans, as far as I could tell, so I figured I had a shot. Every young comic seemed to show up for it. And here I thought I'd been singled out because I was special, or uniquely talented. (I would have even settled for funny-smelling, because at least it would have been distinctive.) Some of the people auditioning weren't even comics. There were a number of black actors, for example, and I remember thinking the odds were against them. I mean, there was probably only one African-American spot in the cast, so you figure it out. And yet everywhere you turned backstage there were all these black actors rehearsing monologues from *Raisin in the Sun,* and hoping for the best.

I don't know that I killed when my turn finally came around, but I like to think I maimed. At the very least, I was abrasive enough to cause a rash, or a mild discoloration. I must have left some sort of mark because the producers called me back a time or two, and eventually I got the job. It's like they were reluctant to give it to me, the way they kept calling me back, like they wanted to be double-sure they weren't about to make a horrible mistake.

People are always asking me about my one season on *Saturday Night Live,* but only after they read my bio or my Wikipedia page, because nobody remembers the season itself. My own asshole agent, even. (The first one, not the new-and-improved one.) No, she's not my agent anymore, but she certainly was at the time. She once called me very excitedly, before the agency people got around to firing her, to tell me she got me an audition for *Saturday Night Live,* and I had to explain to her that I had already been on the show, and that I'd already been fired.

This was news to her.

Last I heard of her, my asshole agent was working as a real estate agent, which may explain the homeless problem.

My asshole agents aside—a transitional phrase that works doubly well for me and my asides—I became known in certain circles as the untalented guy with the irritating voice from the worst season of *Saturday Night Live*. It's not exactly the best nickname in the world, and it's difficult to imagine it fitting on a T-shirt. This was just as well, I always thought, because it's nice to be known in certain circles, especially concentric ones. In truth, most people had no idea I was on the show, and the ones who did have a vague recollection of my hardly memorable contribution couldn't seem to keep track of all the different incarnations of the show and its cast.

This was understandable. By this point, after so many years and so many cast members, looking back at the history of *Saturday Night Live* is like watching one of those prehistoric movies where cavemen are battling dinosaurs. There is a little time lapse of several million years between cavemen and dinosaurs, but that never got in the way of a good story. It's the same thing with *Saturday Night Live*. Pointing to one bad season is a little like referring to the issue of *Playboy* with the naked girl in it, so I sometimes mess with people's heads when the subject comes up, just to see if they're paying attention. They'll ask me about the show, and I'll tell them about the cast. I'll mention some people from the original cast, some people from the current cast, some people from the cast of *Bridget Loves Bernie* . . . whatever comes to mind. They'll nod politely, and smile knowingly, and tell me they remember it like it was yesterday. I'll say, "My favorite was the recurring character I played on those Leeping Skeet-shooter sketches." And they'll say it was their favorite, too.

Now, here's another point of pause, for another show business observation: do you know how people are always saying you should go out of your way to be nice to the people you meet on your way up, because they're the same people you're going to meet on the way down? It's such a cliché, and you hear it all the time—not just in show business, but everywhere. But I learned early on that it's a load of crap. Here's my feeling on the matter: be as big a creep as you want to be to people you meet on your way up, because if you're on your way up people want to be your friend no matter what. If you're on your way down, nobody cares how nice you used to be.

Words to live by, don't you think?

Once again, I return you to our regularly scheduled story . . .

I started at *Saturday Night Live* with Joe Piscopo, Eddie Murphy, and a whole bunch of people you've probably never even heard of. Most of us were fired midway through our one and only season—the show's sixth, if you're keeping score—although Joe and Eddie were allowed to hang around for a while, which worked out well for me because as Eddie became more famous he was in a better position to hire me in *Beverly Hills Cop II*. And, as Joe became more famous, he was in a better position to hire me to rub body oil on him for one of his muscle magazine photo shoots.

As it happened, that *Beverly Hills Cop II* gig had nothing to do with Eddie Murphy. I got hired the regular way—by auditioning and whining and crossing my fingers. There was no nod or nudge from my old pal Eddie. In fact, when I turned up on set for my scenes, Eddie came over and told me how surprised he was to see me there. He said, "We used to work together, right? You seem vaguely familiar."

People still come up to me on the street to talk about *Beverly Hills Cop II.* They do my scenes, word-for-word, which I always find interesting because those word-for-words weren't in the script. We improvised the whole thing. I played an accountant. The way it was written, it was a very straightforward scene—and by *straightforward* I mean straight. For some reason, I ended up playing it gay. To this day, I don't know why. Also, I don't know that anyone noticed, except me.

(If you want to know the truth, neither one of us wanted to play it straight. We talked about this, me and Eddie Murphy. We thought gay would be so much better, but unfortunately we didn't have the budget for a lavish musical number.)

In the original scene, Eddie Murphy's character went to the accountant to take care of some traffic tickets. One of my lines was, "Is there some way we can avoid this unpleasantness?" It wasn't a very funny line, even though it seemed to sum up my approach to life and work, so we went another way with it. At the end of the scene, in the part that always gets the biggest laugh, my accountant character yells "Bitch!" into the phone, only now when the movie is shown on television the word has been edited out. Apparently, you can show the crack of someone's ass, or make hardly veiled references to sexual activity or bodily functions, but you can't scream "Bitch!" into a telephone.

I knew Joe Piscopo from the comedy clubs, but I don't remember meeting Eddie before *Saturday Night Live.* Looking back, I suppose it's possible that I might have seen Eddie at some of the clubs, but I might have him confused with one of the busboys. It's not politically correct, and I'm ashamed to admit it, but black people and Asians do all look alike to me. In all fairness to me, and to Eddie, it might have been Sidney Poitier.

Somewhere along the way, *Saturday Night Live* went beyond funny or unfunny. Now it's just a restaurant in a good location. Back when I signed on, it was considered an outrage that a group of unknowns was trying to replace the original cast of "Not Ready for Prime-Time Players," a moniker that might have been wryly amusing for a while but seemed to lose its relevance over the years. Nowadays, the cast changes between commercial breaks, but at the time it was considered a call to war. It was as if in the middle of Beatlemania someone announced that John, Paul, George and Ringo were being replaced by four new guys, and that one of them would be an impish Jew with an irritating voice who would hardly appear onstage—like Ringo, I guess, without the Jewish part.

The silver lining to my cometlike appearance on *Saturday Night Live* was that I now had a track record. It wasn't a particularly good track record, and it certainly wasn't a long one, but this didn't seem to bother casting agents and producers. At least, it didn't bother them after a while. I didn't work a whole lot right after I was fired, and I drifted back to the New York comedy club scene, where I resumed my role as the guy in the back of the room the emcee kept failing to notice when he was searching for another few comics to put on before closing. But then a certain amount of time passed and people in a position to hire me conveniently forgot that there had been a stigma attached to me, following that disastrous *Saturday Night Live* season. Or maybe the topical ointment my doctor had prescribed to relieve the stigma had finally started to work. However it happened, and however long it took, I came to realize that casting agents and producers liked that I had been on television, that's all. This way, if I screwed up mightily, they could at least point to my résumé and say, "Hey, he was on *Saturday Night Live*. How the hell was I supposed to know he works with a drool cup?"

After *Saturday Night Live,* I went from being a complete unknown to a famous failure. The standard line of rejection I used to hear went from, "I'm not hiring Gilbert Gottfried, I don't know who he is" to "I know all too well who Gilbert Gottfried is and I'm not hiring him."

In Hollywood, work leads to work. Maybe not right away, but eventually. And maybe not by design, but it just kind of happens. A role in one film leads to a role in another, which was how *Beverly Hills Cop II* led to *Look Who's Talking Too* and *Problem Child 2*. (I was big in sequels, although I somehow managed to sneak into the cast of the first *Problem Child* movie, which many critics believed was a pale imitation of the sequel.) Sometimes, you can get hired and rehired simply because the director remembers working with you before and that you were not too objectionable.

Sometimes, too, you can get hired and rehired simply because you're the right size. You don't even have to look especially appealing or right for the part. For *Problem Child*, for example, I had to do a scene in an orphanage with a group of nuns. As so often happens, when we have to do a scene in an orphanage with a group of nuns, there was a lot of blocking and staging and a whole bunch of other nonsense going on before we could actually start shooting. This meant that because of the child labor laws in Hollywood the kid who'd been hired to play the title role couldn't be on the set for all that blocking and staging, so the producers hired a dwarf to play the part, since the cameras weren't rolling anyway. The stand-in dwarf was the same height as the child actor playing the lead, so the lighting would be right.

Well, this was by no means a cute dwarf. He was simply the right size. That was his main qualification. The cute, good-looking dwarfs worked in the A pictures. We had this guy. He was so ugly, he'd scare an Oompa Loompa—one of those dwarfs you'd only find in a nightmare sequence in a pretentious art film. He was bowlegged, with an enormous head, a twisted spine and a mouth that didn't really close. And that was when you looked at him from his good side. So this ugly dwarf was our stand-in Problem Child, and we all went about our business—because, after all, we were consummate professionals. Not just mere professionals, mind you, but consummate professionals, which I think has something to do with soup.

The assistant director on *Problem Child* was a very proper Brit, with a clipped, cultured accent. He always sounded like he was reciting Shakespeare. He'd announce, "Stand close by. We're taking a five-minute break, and then we'll be doing Scene 27, in the cafeteria." Whatever he had to say, all the actors and technicians would sit listening to him like he was Laurence Olivier and we were at some play at the Old Vic.

One afternoon, the assistant director was going on and on

about some important matter. Whatever it was, he made it sound so lovely. I happened to be standing near the terrifically ugly dwarf, who at one point threw up his hands in despair and said, "Boy, if I had that guy's voice, I could get all the pussy I want."

I heard that and thought, *Only in Hollywood*. Then I went back to my dressing room to work on my British accent.

Oh, wait, I just remembered another *Problem Child* anecdote. This one might even be funnier than the one I just told you, so try to put that one out of your mind. This one is from the sequel, *Problem Child 2*, not to be confused with *Look Who's Talking Too*, in which I danced with John Travolta. (He stills calls me. He just won't accept that it's over between us.) I guess that makes this the sequel to my first *Problem Child* anecdote. Anyway, in *Problem Child 2*, there's a big food fight scene in a restaurant. Maybe you remember it. Maybe you don't. But trust me, it's in there somewhere. John Ritter's character is in the scene with his son, Junior, the Problem Child. My character, Mr. Peabody, shows up with an impossibly hot-looking, six-foot-tall model/actress-type. The girl is wearing an outfit to show off her quite magnificent cleavage. (I was going to say *majestic* cleavage, but I wasn't sure how to spell it. Plus, I thought it would be overstating.) However you choose to describe her breasts (I called them Abbott and Costello, if you must know), I gave them much more attention than I gave the script.

So there I was, admiring the work of Laurel and Hardy, when I looked up and saw we were on a break. The writers were huddled with the director on a corner of the set, having a powwow. Me, I was standing off by myself, having a teepee. This went on for quite some time, until the writers and director called the cast back together and told us they had come up with a way to improve the scene. From the excited looks on their faces, I could only imagine that they'd come up with the most brilliant, most scathingly funny bit and that in a year or so we'd all be backstage at the Oscars, congratulating each other on our Academy Awards. So here's what they decided: the food fight would be much funnier if the Problem Child got it started by throwing a meatball at my comely co-star, which was supposed to land squarely between Leopold and Loeb.* Naturally, every prop guy on the set volunteered to be the one standing over Simon and Garfunkel to make sure that the meatball hit its mark—which basically meant standing over this well-chested actress and dropping a meatball between her tits.

Now, I don't know anything about the emotional depth of meatballs, but my guess is this one was the happiest meatball in the world. We were all pretty happy, as I recall. It was a good day to be a movie star, and I was overcome with gratitude for being included. And so, in the spirit of collaboration, which is something that I think the art of film is all about, I mustered up my most serious, intelligent, creative-sounding voice and said to the director, "I feel like this scene needs one more beat to make it really work." Then I suggested,

---

* This footnote is for readers who might be unfamiliar with the work of Leopold and Loeb, two famous college students who were known as "the thrill killers" in the 1920s, after kidnapping and murdering a little boy in what they thought would go down as the perfect crime. I include this information so readers will understand the reference, and enjoy the full humor of the piece. Also, I'm told that writers who use footnotes in their books come across as particularly smart and scholarly, so I'm going for that as well.

unselfishly, that once the meatball finds its mark, my character should reach down between my co-star's breasts and try to get the meatball out.

The director considered this for a moment, and then flashed me a look that I took to mean, *Aha! This is why we hire someone like Gottfried. For his dedication to the craft of filmmaking.*

And so it was agreed that I would stick my hand down this actress's top and dig out the meatball. Being the perfectionist that I've always been, we did the scene several times that day, with me shoving my hands inside and outside and all over my co-star's monumental breasts—or, let's just call them Hall and Oates. For some reason, I was never fully happy with any of my performances, and kept insisting we do another take. I was determined to get it right.

Finally, at Take 187, the director yelled, "Cut! That's a print!"

I knew better than to go against my director, and yet I objected strongly, because I felt there was still more I could do with the scene, and suggested instead that perhaps another meatball thrown into the actress's twat would really punch up the picture. The director didn't see it quite the same way. He seemed to admire my stick-to-itiveness, but he insisted that it was time to move on to the next scene—although if he'd agreed to try out my meatball-in-the-twat idea, I would have offered to pay overtime for the crew.

Still, it was a banner day on the *Problem Child 2* set. When we broke, the director took me aside, put his arm around my shoulders and complimented me on my professionalism. He said, "To do the scene so many times, Gilbert, without complaining . . . it's a marvelous thing."

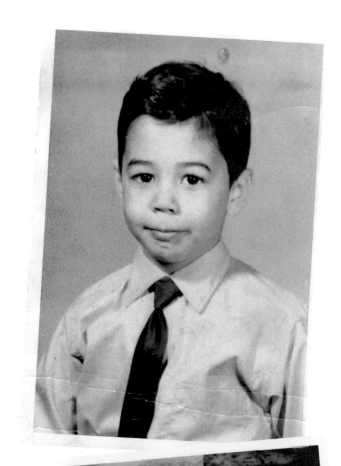

ABOVE: An elementary school photo. Sometimes I take this picture out, look at it, and say, "Damn, you'd think I would have wound up a lot better looking." *(Courtesy of the author)*

AT RIGHT: Me at a young age, taking my aggressions out with my sister, Arlene. *(Courtesy of the author)*

ABOVE LEFT: Teenage Gilbert wondering if the police would find the bodies buried under the floorboards. *(Arlene Gottfried)*

ABOVE RIGHT: Damn, I should have been a rock star. *(Arlene Gottfried)*

AT RIGHT: Early 8 x 10 with me looking like a Mexican migrant farmworker. *(Arlene Gottfried)*

BELOW: Me at Improv doing a bit about Jesus. (Yes, my people killed him.) *(Courtesy of the author)*

ABOVE: Not sure what I was doing in this photo. Probably auditioning to play Tevye in *Fiddler on the Roof*. *(Arlene Gottfried)*

AT RIGHT: As Groucho Marx on *Thicke of the Night*. *(Courtesy of the author)*

BELOW: Young Jew comic with old Jew comic Henny "King of the One-Liners" Youngman. *(Courtesy of the author)*

ABOVE LEFT: Of course, erect, it would have been bigger. *(Arlene Gottfried)*

ABOVE RIGHT: Performing at a fund-raiser for the Nazi Party. *(Arlene Gottfried)*

AT LEFT: *The Adventures of Ford Fairlane.* I think the blood on my face is from the battering we took from the critics. *(Courtesy of the author)*

BELOW: I don't know Charlie Sheen, but I figured if I said "Hi" he might want to share some drugs and hookers with me. *(Courtesy of the author)*

TOP: With Gene Wilder and Richard Pryor while filming the laughless *Another You*. I wound up on the cutting-room floor. *(Courtesy of the author)*

BOTTOM: *Problem Child*. Posing with John Ritter before he died (after he died would have been just plain inappropriate). *(Courtesy of the author)*

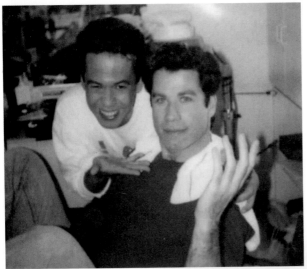

TOP: I danced with John Travolta in *Look Who's Talking Too*. He won't stop calling me. *(Courtesy of the author)*

BOTTOM: I can honestly say Mei Dick does very well in Chinatown. *(Arlene Gottfried)*

TOP: Bubbie and me. *(Arlene Gottfried)*

ABOVE: Me, proudly busting out of the
crapper, backstage at *The Tonight Show.*
(Courtesy of the author)

AT RIGHT: As Yoda on *The Tonight Show.*
(Courtesy of the author)

TOP LEFT: With Digit, my character on the cartoon *Cyberchase*. *(Courtesy of the author)*

ABOVE: AFLAC!!! *(Courtesy of the author)*

AT LEFT: Not sure what joke I just said, but it's a safe bet it was filthy and offensive. *(David Simon)*

I nodded my head and said, "Well, sir. It's all part of being an artist."

Not everyone appreciated my artistic talents. After I'd been acting in movies for a while, I was promised a part in a big-budget picture, to be written and directed by Warren Beatty. (Or maybe I should rewrite that last sentence to read, "After I'd been *appearing* in movies for a while . . ." because few people considered what I was doing *acting*.) All of A-list Hollywood wanted in on this picture, I was told (especially all the cute, A-list dwarves), but I didn't even have to audition. There was a part in this thing being written especially for me. The picture turned out to be *Dick Tracy,* which wasn't exactly one of Warren Beatty's most successful films. Keep in mind, this was the *Dick Tracy* movie based on the famous Sunday comics detective, and not on the famous children's dick-tracing game where you got out a piece of paper and traced your penis. (As far as I know, they never made a movie out of that, but it was a wonderful game.) The part turned out to be Mumbles, the hard-to-understand henchman of the big crime boss, to be played by Al Pacino. I thought it was a great part for me, because nobody could understand me anyway, and I wouldn't have to work too hard to memorize my lines. However, a few weeks before shooting, my agent called and said they were going to hire someone else.

"So who are they going with?" I quite reasonably wanted to know.

"Dustin Hoffman," my agent said.

This meant that it had come down to the wire between me and Dustin Hoffman, which I could only imagine was just like the time it came down to the wire between me and

Jack Nicholson in *Terms of Endearment*—another part I didn't get. If what my agent told me was true, you could make the argument that I was also close to getting *The Graduate, Midnight Cowboy* and *Tootsie.* I found this hard to believe, although it's possible the call came in offering me the part in *The Graduate* when I was living in my parents' apartment. I seem to remember the phone ringing one afternoon, but I didn't answer it because I was busy at the time. I was jerking off to *Petticoat Junction.* I never actually watched the show, but the title alone was enough to get me going. I mean, a *petticoat?* Who could blame me? I saw it listed in *TV Guide* and I was off and rubbing. You had to take what you could get in those days, because there was no cable.

I also found this hard to believe because in the entire history of the motion picture industry my name and Dustin Hoffman's name have never been mentioned in the same conversation, and I can't imagine that they ever will. Well, strike that: the only way our names would appear together in the same Hollywood conversation would be in the sentence, "I've seen Gilbert Gottfried's acting, and he's no Dustin Hoffman."

So Gilbert Gottfried was out, and Dustin Hoffman was in, which I guess takes us to another common Hollywood expression:

4. *The part is yours, Gilbert Gottfried . . . unless Dustin Hoffman wants it—or anyone else, for that matter.*

Looking back over my "brilliant" career, it's distressing to me (and more than a little perplexing) that I've never done a nude scene. Incredible as it may seem, I've appeared in over a hundred movies and television shows, and I've never once been asked to take off my clothes. Quite the opposite, in fact. Very often, my female co-stars will ask specifically that I keep my clothes on. It's a matter of contract for some of them. Even in some of the animated shows I do, it expressly states that I'd be in violation if I turned up naked on the set.

This is a shame. I would even go so far as to suggest that it's a crying shame, except I'm not quite sure what that is. A shame is shame enough, although I suppose I could cry because I've spent a lot of time thinking about this, and a lot of time preparing. Really, I've made a careful study of Hollywood nude scenes, and I believe I'd be quite good at one. I can only imagine that sex in movies is an accurate reflection of sex in real life, although I must confess that I haven't had any of one and hardly enough of the other to pass myself off as anything of an authority. Let's just say I'm a fan. I understand that there must be a good reason why Neve Campbell does a three-way while wearing a bra the whole time, because that must mirror real life. I understand that you need to light hundreds and hundreds of scented candles to help establish the proper mood (and, I suppose, the proper scent), because everyone I know just happens to have hundreds and hundreds of scented candles lying about the house for just this purpose. I understand how A-list actresses wake up in bed with some guy and the blanket is magically tucked beneath her armpits and clutched to her chest, because one time I was fortunate enough to have sex with a woman who was mildly attractive and she was so ashamed of herself afterward she couldn't even look at herself in a mirror. That blanket stuck to her body like there was suction involved. Or if there's no blanket, an actress will get up and cross the room with the entire bedsheet draped around her like an evening gown. And I understand all about bubble baths, too, because everything is covered, and you can reach for an oversized towel while you're still in the water and wrap it all the way around in such a way that not a single naughty bit might see the light of day—or, the light of a soundstage.

I've been practicing getting out of bathtubs like this for years, in case it should ever come up, but only with mixed results. Another Hollywood bubble bath trick that seems to have eluded me is the way some adventurous actresses emerge from the tub without a towel, and yet the bubbles have somehow formed themselves into a bikini. I've practiced this, too, but it doesn't seem to work on me. Maybe I'm doing something wrong. I just stand there wet and naked and cold, wondering how I might get the bubbles to form themselves into a warm towel.

A classic Hollywood bedroom maneuver is a little move I like to call the *drop-and-sigh*, which happens with great frequency after a scene that's meant to tastefully show an exhilarating round of wild sex. Have you noticed this, or is it just me? The camera pans away to show the pillows by the headboard, and then there's a wave of husky, celebratory noises we can only assume are meant to signal an orgasm, and then suddenly the spent and satisfied couple falls back onto the pillows in a two-shot, side-by-side. Typically, their heads hit the pillow at exactly the same moment, and each time I'm left wondering how these spent and satisfied people have managed to enjoy their wild Hollywood sex in a side-by-side manner. I suppose it's possible that, as stars, they have an extra set of sex organs on their hips, which makes a certain amount of sense. I mean, movie stars don't just become famous for no apparent reason.

One of my favorite movie modesty moments came in a scene with Phoebe Cates, who appeared to be diddling herself onscreen with a piece of black electrical tape covering one of her nipples. I won't mention the title of the movie, to protect its privacy. (Oh, wait a second . . . Phoebe Cates wasn't diddling herself in the scene, after all. That was me, watching the scene.) The black electrical tape was a little beside the point, don't you think? What, did Phoebe Cates tell her agent she didn't mind appearing in such a suggestive manner, but she drew the line at appearing topless?

The most likely explanation, of course, is that Phoebe Cates wasn't modest at all, but was instead experiencing some sort of short circuit in her tits on the day of filming, and that there were sparks flying out of her nipples. The black electrical tape was just a precaution.

Now, I'm not complaining. I enjoy an artfully placed piece of electrical tape as much as the next guy. I even enjoy the thought of side-by-side sex, between two consenting stars, or the adhering properties of a well-bubbled bath. I'm just taking notes, studying the standards and practices of the industry, waiting for my chance to step in and shine. Yes, I remain at the ever-ready, even after all these years, at my advanced age. My thinking is, if Hume Cronyn and Don Ameche and Wilford Brimley can be applauded for appearing nearly naked in *Cocoon*, then I'll get my chance to appear nearly naked before long. I'm just waiting for the right role.

Of course, I won't just do nudity for the sake of doing nudity. It has to be integral to my character. It has to serve the story, because I have a problem with gratuitous nudity—unless of course I'm sitting in a dark theater with a raincoat over my lap.

Here's a curious, little-known fact: I still have a Tic Tac in my shirt pocket from my very first movie, a little piece of crap I did in 1984 called *The House of God*, with Tim Matheson, Bess Armstrong, Joe Piscopo, and Sandra Bernhard. Such a cast! Even Michael Richards was in this thing. And . . . nothing! All this time later . . . still nothing. I've worked with all these beautiful stars, and all I've got to show for it is an excruciating case of celebrity blue balls.

This has been especially frustrating, considering the Tic Tac. Put me in one of these teen vampire movies and I'd be all over the young undead starlet, and she'd remark on my fresh, clean breath, although I have to think that original Tic-Tac has emulsified by this point and lost some of its effectiveness, which is interesting because the role would probably call for me to take my shirt off and flex my considerable abs, which might very possibly lead my comely co-star to remark about my luminous, even-toned skin. However, this would also mean that my shirt would be back in my dressing room, and I'd be too entranced by my Method acting approach to collect the Tic Tac from the pocket before heading out to the set, so maybe it's just as well.

As long as I'm on it, let me just tie together a few loose strands from the front end of my career. My first movie led to a second and then to a third, although I chose to skip the fourth, fifth and sixth movies offered to me because they'd been talking to Woody Allen and wanted me to play a Navajo Indian, but then I took the next one, which I guess was officially my seventh movie even though it was really only my fourth, and after that things proceeded along in fits and starts. Sometimes a director would look at me when I turned up on the set for my day or two of filming and say, "Oh, Gilbert, are you in this?"

I'd hear that and think, *At least he recognizes me.* Then I'd ask him if he wanted me to take my clothes off and things would generally go downhill from there.

Clip 'n' Save Joke no. 6 ✂--------

A man places a call to the law firm of Goldstein, Goldstein, Goldstein & Goldstein. "Is Mr. Goldstein in?" he asks. "I'd like to speak with him about a legal matter."

"He's not in today," comes the reply. "He's away on vacation."

"Very well," the man says. "Can I please speak with Mr. Goldstein instead?"

"He's out to lunch," the man is told.

"How about Mr. Goldstein?" the man tries again. "Is he in?"

"Yes, but I'm afraid he's in a meeting," the voice on the other end informs him.

The potential client is frustrated, but he tries one final time. "Okay, then," he says. "Is Mr. Goldstein available?"

"Speaking."

6

First Impressions, Lasting Tributes

I'm known for my impressions. I don't mean to blow smoke up my own ass, but ever since Mayor Bloomberg made it so difficult to smoke in New York City, I'm having a hard time finding someone to pucker up and do it for me. Plus, I'm the kind of guy who likes to call a spade a spade, even if it pisses him off and he winds up beating the crap out of me in some alley.

In all fairness to me—and, to belabor the same damn point, this is my book so it's only natural that I tend to favor the author—I've always had an ear for voices, which is a whole lot more practical for a comic than having a face for voice-overs, and one of the ideas behind this book is to share my many gifts and body parts with my loyal fans. This has been my credo, for as long as I can remember having a credo. To share my gifts and body parts. Freely, and often. It's my reason for being, if you will. And, now that I've taken up the pen—which, in case you were wondering, is not *really* mightier than most swords (it's just an expression, apparently)—it's my reason for writing as well. It's my own little writer's credo. If I had a desk, and if I was the sort of writer inclined to work at it, instead of just scribbling away on loose scraps of paper while I ride the subway, I might even print out this credo on a plaque or one of those desk nameplates and display it prominently, for inspiration. But that's not about to happen, so I'll just scribble it down and make note of it.

A writer is supposed to write what he knows, right? Well, I know voices. It's uncanny, the thing I have with voices, and I mean to share it with you here, dear reader.

Also, I'm told that my writing style resembles that of Judy Blume, the famous Young Adult novelist who writes about cramps and pimples and not being invited to the prom, and Onslow Stevens, the long-dead and little-remembered American character actor who appeared in *House of Dracula* opposite Lon Chaney, Jr. I mention Onslow Stevens in this context because I can't help myself, and his appearance here in an aside meant to accentuate a small piece of preamble that will soon enough take us to a longer, more sustained bit comes with an unexpected bonus. You see, I have an Onslow Stevens story.

Now, it's not every day that you come across a conversation starter like that one: *I have an Onslow Stevens story.* To be sure, we all have our Onslow Stevens stories, but since I seem to have the floor I'll share mine here. When I was in elementary school, in first or second grade, the teacher decided to fill the time by having us name famous people to correspond with various sets of initials. When she worked her way around the room to me, I had to come up with a name to match the initials O.S. So of course I blurted out a name that would have been on the tips of first- or second-grade tongues all across this great land: Onslow Stevens.

What the hell did she expect me to say? Oskar Schindler?

He hadn't even started his acting career yet, so how was I supposed to know who he was? O. J. Simpson? He hadn't even started his killing people career yet, or his running through airports career, so that pretty much left Onslow Stevens. I was just five or six, but good ol' Onslow was the O.S. to end all O.S.'s, if you asked me.

And so, back to my Judy Blume–Onslow Stevens writing style. This is a good and winning combination, I'm told by my publishers, because apparently Young Adult–type people seem to enjoy books about pimples and vampires.

Ah, kids these days . . .

But every writer has his own style. However, in this part of the book I won't be focusing on style. No, the emphasis here will be on my God-given and self-nurtured talent for brilliant mimicry. (*Self-nurturing* . . . another one of my strengths, but that's for another chapter.)

Read on, and you'll get what I mean . . .

Here I am, doing Jack Nicholson:

"You can't handle the truth."

Wow. What more can I say? Just in case you were wondering, again, that impression was spot-on. A virtuoso performance. I really, really nailed it. Sounded just like him. You'll just have to trust me on this. Granted, that impression would be a whole lot funnier if you could just imagine me pounding my fist in an emphatic way on the witness stand, which for comedic purposes could be made of simple pine instead of the traditional walnut or mahogany. Or, even funnier, you can picture me and my Jack Nicholson impression out of context. That's always an effective comedic twist. In comedy graduate school, it's known as juxtaposition. In my doctoral thesis, I even referred to this technique as desperation—or, in academic terms, "trying anything and hoping it works." It's been the basis for my entire career, so I might as well reach for it here. Let's say we're walking into a pizza place and we're hungry for a slice. Let's also say that the guy behind the counter has some difficulty "handling" our order, so we lean in and pound our fist in an emphatic way on the glass counter, to make ourselves understood.

Got it? Good, now let's try it again:

"You can't handle the truth."

Not bad, huh? Pure comedy gold, if you ask me. And, if you ask the guy sitting next to me on the subway, reading over my shoulder.

Now imagine that I'm Al Pacino and I'm heading into a car rental place, looking for a subcompact. Here goes:

"Say hello to my little friend."

To make it even better, dear reader, it helps if I'm sweating profusely as I say this, and for me to have a tiny bit of spittle flying from the corner of my mouth, and for me to pronounce *little* as *leeeetle*, in true *Scareface* mode.

Pretty fucking funny, right?

Like I said, uncanny.

I've also got another Al Pacino impression up my comedy sleeve. Think of it like a two-for-one deal. You pay for the book, expecting just the one Al Pacino impression, and I overwhelm you with a second. That's a real value, if you ask me.

Ready? Here goes: *"Hooo aaahhh!"*

Notice, dear reader, that my follow-up "homage" to Al Pacino features an extra *"o"* at the front end, and an extra little surprise at the back end. Most hack comedians, they do Al Pacino in *Scent of a Woman,* they go, *"Hoo ha!"* But they're wrong. Be assured, my way is correct, and for a treat I toss in that extra *"o"* in the *"Hooo"* part. And there's no hard *"h"* sound at the front of the *"aaahhh"* part.

I choose to slather it on pretty thick, because nothing's too good for my fans. I make the extra-effort. My comedy recipes are made with the finest ingredients. I give, and then I give some more: *"Hooo aaahhh!"*

(And, as a bonus, I show admirable restraint in avoiding any snide comments about one of the most unfortunately titled movies in the Al Pacino canon, which invariably turns up on several lists of all-time titles of mainstream movies that could be mistaken for porn movies. It's right up there with *Reservoir Dogs* and *The Last Temptation of Christ,* don't you think?)

I could go on and on with these groundbreaking, print-equivalent impressions—and I guess I will, because in comedy parlance this is what's known as being on a roll, which of course is not to be confused with the subcategory of comedy parlance that refers specifically to a series of successful jokes about World War II (being on a *Kaiser roll*).

Next: Marlon Brando, from *Apocalypse Now*—and for this one it helps to imagine me with a fat, bald head, emerging in half-shadow from the heart of an unimaginable darkness, somewhere deep in the jungle. Close your eyes and picture it. Okay: *"Oh, the horror!"*

It's a gift, I know, but I'm only too happy to share it here, dear reader. That's what I do, I share. I'm a giver. It's my nature. Also, I'm a cutting edge kind of giver. As far as I know—which, frankly, isn't very far—I'm the first comedian to even attempt doing voices on the page, so I'm figuring it out as I go along. We're all in on the ground floor of this literary innovation, and I suppose it might punch things up a bit if I do a little comedic sleight of hand before each impression. I'm open to suggestions, to trying new things. Where you're on a roll, like I am here, you're too busy concentrating on rolling, and then (relatedly) on not getting sick from all that rolling, so you don't always take the time to tweak. But that's not me. I take the time. I tweak. There's always room for improvement, right? So indulge me a moment, while I give myself some notes. First, I should turn around, my back to the audience, as I get into character. Then I should make all these elaborate gestures to suggest that I'm fixing my hair, tugging on my collar, transforming myself into the person I'm about to impersonate. Like Rich Little used to do, only bigger.

Dustin Hoffman, in *Rain Man*: *"I'm an excellent driver."*

As a comic sweetener, imagine if you will that Dustin Hoffman is about to board the *Back to the Future* roller-coaster ride at Universal Studios in Orlando, Florida, after waiting on an unusually long line, beneath an unseasonably hot midday sun. All around him, the Universal Studios patrons are disgruntled and restless and a bit out of sorts, after such a long wait, but not Dustin Hoffman. All right, that sets the scene. Now jump back up a couple lines and reread my impression as Dustin Hoffman takes his seat in the front of the roller coaster and laugh among yourselves.

I don't just *do* men, by the way.

(Wait, that didn't come out right. I know this because the guy sitting next to me on the subway reading over my shoulder just moved away from me, looking uncomfortable.)

Let me try that one again: I don't just *do* male voices. I also *do* women.

(There, that's more like it.)

And so, for all of you readers who are fans of the fairer sex and old movie classics, here's my Bette Davis impression:

"But you are in the chair, Blanche."

Oh, wait. I forgot to tell you the stage directions. I'm smoking a cigarette as I write this. Repeat.

(For a moment there, I was going to write "Rinse, lather, repeat," but then I realized it was the punch line to some other bit I may or may not get around to writing.)

Meryl Streep, with that wonderfully thick Polish accent she used to such dramatic effect in *Sophie's Choice*: *"Aw, you might as well take the one on the left. He was never going to amount to anything, anyway. Plus, he has his father's nose."*

Sandra Bullock: *"Honey, take your tattooed biker dick out of that stripper's pussy and help me find a place on the shelf for my Oscar!"*

Now, another thing they teach you in comedy graduate school is the big finish, and I'm way ahead of you here. As you can see, I've built up this literary impression routine in such a way that we're now in the middle of a rollicking crescendo, which really is the best kind of *crescendo*, and headed for a grand finale, where I intend to leave you rolling in the aisles. Hopefully, wherever you're reading this, in whatever format, there will be some sort of aisle nearby. I've set it up so you now have no choice but to appreciate my ability to cross genders and genres with my impressions, so you're ready for anything. You are fairly helpless against my powers as an entertainer.

But wait. Before my boffo close, I believe it's important to point out my disinterest in the scene I am about to reinterpret. In fact, I am one of the only people in my acquaintance (and I happen to be one of my very closest acquaintances) who didn't laugh at Meg Ryan's famous *climactic* scene in *When Harry Met Sally*. I didn't even crack a knowing smile. It really didn't do anything for me, that scene. I just didn't get it—but that didn't make it any less memorable.

And so, in rousing conclusion, I offer my virtuoso Meg Ryan impression:

"Oh, oh, oh, oh . . . Mmmmmm . . . Oh, oh, oh, oh . . . Oh Jesus God, no . . . I mean, Oh Jesus God, yes . . . Yes, yes, yes, yes . . . Oh, oh, oh, oh . . . Yes, yes, yes, yes . . ."

And so on. And so forth. And so help me. And, with a little bit of an exclamation point in the form of me pounding my fist on the table in front of me, for emphasis.

Now, in the interest of full disclosure, I should probably mention here that I am physically incapable of faking an orgasm. I know this because I've tried, on many occasions. I haven't had a lot of practice, mind you, but I've made the most of my opportunities. In fact, the few times I've gotten lucky in my life, I was always made to feel it was because God had somehow stopped paying attention. It's like He had to leave the room to go to take a leak, and the world tilted on its axis in such a way that my pants fell to my ankles and the girl I was with at the time didn't run from the room in horror. Either way, God or no God, it hasn't come up all that often, but I'm pretty sure I can't fake an orgasm.

Women seem to have no problem in this area, especially around me. Sometimes, they're so disinterested, they don't even bother faking. They just tell me to go away. Me, I can fake an erection, but for some reason my orgasms are almost always authentic, and the "impersonation" of Meg Ryan's fake orgasm in a Jewish deli that you just enjoyed a brief moment ago falls into the authentic category, I'm afraid. Yes, that was really me, coming. All over the place, I was coming, which probably makes this the first time in recent publishing history when it was a good thing to be reading a book in one of those newfangled digital formats, because as far as I know it's impossible for my ejaculate to travel from my own handheld device to yours.

Lucky for you, the technology isn't quite there yet. But it will be, soon. And when it is, I'll be all over it. Or, I should say, I'll be all over *you*.

Clip 'n' Save Joke no. 7 ✂

A middle-aged man is taking a walk in the country. All of a sudden, he hears a voice calling out to him. He hears, "Sir, can you please help me?" He looks down and sees that the voice is coming from a frog.

Now that it has the man's attention, the frog thinks it might be a good idea to explain itself. The frog says, "At one time I was the most beautiful princess in all the land. A witch cast a spell on me and turned me in to a frog. If you kiss me, it will turn me back into the ravishingly beautiful princess I used to be, and in return I will have the most amazing, most mind-blowing sex with you that you've ever experienced in your life. We will do this in every position and manner possible."

So the man picks up the frog and puts it in his pocket. Then he continues on his way. After a while, the frog sticks its head out and says, "Aren't you going to kiss me, so I can turn back into a beautiful princess and have amazing sex with you?"

"No," the man says. "At my age I'd rather have a talking frog."

7

Adventures in Animation

Okay, so that pretty much covers the front end of my career. It's the rear end that gives me trouble.

Let's just say my career has walked a tightrope between early-morning children's programming and hardcore porn. I remarked on this once in an interview, in an offhanded way, which is how I do most of my remarking when I give interviews. But then I realized that many a truth is said in jest, sometimes in an offhanded way. I know this because I read it in a fortune cookie.

Say what you will about my career (and, frankly, I'm satisfied when someone says *anything* about my career), there's no denying that sometime after those first few movies and those early fits and starts I came to occupy a creepy place on the spectrum of mildly popular culture. How this happened—or, when; or, why—I've got no idea, only that it seems to have been a happy accident, because I'm quite certain I never dreamed of a career in show business that walked a tightrope between early-morning children's programming and hard-core porn. It just worked out that way. You see, it turned out that I have a face for voice-overs. That line is not original to

me, of course. Every schmuck who's ever worked in radio
has used a version of that line to appear self-deprecating and
humble, but I'm borrowing it here because I really do have a
face for voice-overs.

(For what it's worth, and it's probably not much, I tend
to avoid self-deprecation and humility, unless they involve
some form of direct compensation.)

I know this because some Disney executive once told me it
wouldn't be such a good idea to show my face in public at a
Disney event or to appear at one of their theme parks because
I might frighten small children. This was discussed at the corporate level, apparently, and there was General Consensus—
and who am I to question General Consensus? Up and down
the chain of command, it's a different story. Corporal Punishment? Him I can second-guess. Private Parts? Also, open
to scrutiny. Major Disappointment? Ah, this fellow keeps
turning up, without fail, every time I speak into a microphone, and of course I can't be expected to keep from ques-
tioning *him*. But General Consensus? No, he knows his stuff.

Not to mention Sergeant Flea Collar . . .

(By the way, what the hell kind of phrase is *not to mention*?
Think about it: those words never appear in a sentence unless whatever it is that's not quite worthy of mention is in fact
being mentioned. But it's a resilient little phrase. You can be
on the lookout for it, and guarding against it, and it can still
sneak its way into your sentences when you're looking the
other way—as I have apparently been doing here. I can't tell
you how broken up I am about this.)

Back to that thing I wasn't about to mention: Sergeant
Flea Collar, for those of you too young or too disinterested

to remember, was a promotional character developed by the Sergeant line of pet products, and it's hardly worth mentioning here except that it amuses me to do so. My thinking here is, *To hell with you, dear reader, if you choose not to join me in my amusement.* But that's entirely up to you.

Actually, now that I've gone and not-about-to-mentioned it, I'm a little fuzzy on this one. Let's just say I *think* Sergeant Flea Collar was a promotional character, but I can't be certain. If it wasn't, it should have been. At the very least, if it wasn't, those Sergeant people really missed out on an opportunity— and I could have made a buck doing the voice-over.

If memory serves—and here I am almost certain that it does; not only that, it also cleans up after itself—the first voice-over role I ever auditioned for was the part of the wisecracking parrot Iago in the animated Disney feature *Aladdin*. I was born to play that role, it turns out. To this day, it stands as one of the defining moments of my career, which even I have to admit is somewhat sad.

(Check that: I don't *have* to admit it, but I believe that doing so makes me somewhat more attractive to women—or, at least, to the sort of women who might not find the idea of a short, foul-mouthed Jewish comedian admitting to a slight professional regret to be not too terribly repulsive.)

One thing led to another, and after that toward some other thing that was neither here nor there, and after that I was headed off on this whole new career path that would never have presented itself if I hadn't gotten this Disney job. Now all these years later I'm known for playing this wisecracking parrot, and for telling the world's filthiest joke—two crowning achievements, to which I must also add the appearance of my bald, misshapen head bursting through my mother's vagina during childbirth (technically speaking, my first crowning achievement, according to official records). Not incidentally, it was at just this moment, family historians have noted, that I uttered my first word—"Aflac!"—which came out sounding like a whiny, nasally honk, and after that the OB-GYN turned to my mother and said, "I think you might have something here!"

I can no longer recall with any reliable degree of certainty if I knew I was reading for the role of a cartoon character when I went out on that *Aladdin* audition. It's possible that I asked my agent what I should wear, but I don't think so. If you've seen my wardrobe, you'll know there's no point in even asking.

("Oh, *pants?* You think?")

But it became apparent to me soon enough that I was reading for the voice of a cartoon parrot. Certainly, by the second act. Afterward, I heard one of the Disney executives who'd been sitting in on my audition turn to one of his colleagues and say, "Gilbert Gottfried? I don't know. He always struck me as a little one-dimensional."

Really.

I could only imagine at the time who I was up against for the role—De Niro? Duvall?—but it appeared that they weren't born to it the way I had been born to it. I later learned that it came down to me, Joe Pesci and Danny DeVito. Apparently, the call was out in Hollywood for short, unattractive Jews and Italians. Eventually the part went to me, and once it did I was determined to do a good job with it.

(Years later, I heard it on good authority that the producers had originally offered the part of Iago to Warren Beatty, who turned it down because the thought of playing a parrot in the desert reminded him of his role in *Ishtar*. I have no idea if this is true, but I was raised to believe that a book of comic reminiscences is incomplete without at least one *Ishtar* reference, even if it appears in a parenthetical aside.)

(Moreover, if the parenthetical *Ishtar* reference appears in a stand-alone paragraph, I'm told it can be especially funny.)

I kept asking the *Aladdin* director to help me with my motivation. I wanted to know everything I could about my character, just like they tell you to do in those Method acting classes. This would be my method, I decided, now that I was finally working in a major role, in a major release, from a major studio. It didn't matter that it was a cartoon. It didn't matter that it was a supporting role. At least, I told myself these things didn't matter. In truth, they mattered a great deal. The entire business was like dreaming of being a ballplayer and waking up one day with your balls cupped in your hand and thinking you'd somehow arrived. Still, this was my big break, and I wasn't about to fuck it up. Not if I could help it. Some people might say I was a perfectionist, but that's just me. (Meaning, of course, that it would just be me, saying I was a perfectionist.) At one point, I think I even threw up my hands, and the pages of my script went flying all over the place, and I stormed off the soundstage screaming, "My character would never say such a thing!"

At some other point, immediately following, I think I heard someone ask if Joe Pesci might still be available.

The thing about voice-overs is you're never made to feel like you're working on a movie. You're just standing in a room, reading your lines into a microphone. It's like having a telephone conversation, with a group of earnest people with stopwatches looking on, and no one on the other end of the line. There's no interaction with the other actors, reading the other voices. There's no dressing room, because of course there's no dressing. There's no fancy catering truck, or craft services table filled with good things to eat. There's no syncing of your voice to the action on the screen. That's all done later, in post. In fact, if I had a dollar for every time I heard some middle-aged techie-type tell me something would be done later, in post, I'd have a lot of dollars—enough, certainly, to eat off the McDonald's "Dollar Value" menu for quite some time, which in turn would probably eliminate the need for the fancy catering truck.

Sometimes, the postproduction stage continues long after the movie has been in theaters. Once, after *Aladdin* had become so ridiculously and unaccountably successful it had spawned a couple sequels and a theme park attraction and a Disney Channel cartoon series, I was called back to the studio to redub a scene. In voice-overs, they call this procedure an ADR, which stands for Automated Dialogue Replacement. For years, I thought it stood for Another Disney Requirement, but I was mistaken. Apparently, that was just the way these Disney executives had been trained to make us voice actors feel, like we were beholden to them for our very existence. And, in many ways, we were.

Here, they wanted me to replace one word in a scene from the cartoon series, after it had already aired. In the scene, Iago the parrot was being chased by a tiger, so he quite reasonably exclaimed, "Let's get out of here! That cat is looking at us like we're kitty chow!"

Now, in the Gilbert Gottfried Method School of Voice-Over Acting, this surely counted as something my character might have said, in just such a situation, but apparently there was a woman somewhere in Middle America who begged to differ. Either she didn't understand Iago's motivation, as the cartoon drama was unfolding, or she was just a complete fucking idiot. I tended to lean toward the latter. What happened, best I could tell, was that this complete fucking idiot was watching the cartoon with her children one afternoon, and misheard my character's line. That's all. She thought I said that the cat was looking at us like we were "titty chow." This was troubling, she wrote in a heated letter to the appropriate Disney executive, because it was potentially confusing to her young children, who might have taken Iago's comment as an offhanded endorsement of a popular product developed for people who kept women's breasts as household pets.

Such is the power of a Middle American woman who believes she and her children have been wronged. And so it fell to yours truly, as a caretaker of the Disney brand, to race back to the studio to redub the scene in such a way that even a stupid person with a hearing problem could take no offense.

The human ear can certainly play tricks on us, and I am reminded here of an amusing miscommunication with a woman I was thinking of hiring to clean my house. At least, *I* found it amusing, and this is the most important thing. The woman was British, with the unlikely name of Cunt. I think she spelled it with a "K," but it felt unnatural to me, so I insisted on spelling it with a "C." After all, we were in America, where we can call a Cunt a Cunt, without fear of reprisal.

This was where the amusing miscommunication came into play, because I suppose it's possible that with her British accent the cleaning lady's name wasn't really Cunt at all. Rather—or, *rawther*, as the Brits were wont to say (and you'll notice here that I've slipped in another Brit-seeming word, *wont*, to suggest that I have an ear for accents and dialects and regional phrasing)—it might have been Kant or Kaunt or Kauliflower, and my ears were just playing tricks on me. Either way, this would-be cleaning lady wasn't particularly qualified for the job, but I ended up hiring her anyway, mostly for the opportunity to chase after her all day and say, "Hey, Cunt, dust that cabinet over there!" Or, "Hey, Cunt, you didn't do such a good job mopping my floor!" Or, "Hey, Cunt, I thought I told you to look me in the eye when I talk to you!"

It was a once-in-a-lifetime opportunity—for *me*, of course, and not necessarily for that Cunt—although looking back I'm a little ashamed of my behavior. Some people might say I was a real prick about it, but I prefer to think of myself as more of an asshole. In my defense, my actions came from an honest mistake. I kept hearing one thing, while my hardly qualified cleaning lady kept saying another. After a while, the poor woman couldn't stand it anymore. She didn't want to give up the job, so she changed her name. I think her name was Jane Cunt, so she changed it to Susan Cunt, and after that there was no longer any confusion.

After *Aladdin,* I was basically typecast. My agent kept putting me up for other talking-cartoon-animal parts, but nobody would hire me. I was even up for the part of a swine in an animated bestiality musical, but it went to Ron Jeremy. They said he had a better affinity for the material. This was just as well, because Disney wasn't done with me just yet. I played Iago in a sequel called *The Return of Jafar,* and then in a sequel to the sequel called *Aladdin and the King of Thieves.* Then I did his voice in a whole bunch of direct-to-video pieces of crap, and video games, and eventually someone asked me to read some material for an animatronic version of the parrot Disney wanted to add to its Tiki Room attraction in the Magic Kingdom.

At some point, sitting by myself in a nondescript sound studio in Manhattan, wearing shorts and cupping my balls in my hand beneath the table and reading from a script with the Disney logo watermarked onto each page, I had to pinch myself. For the first time in my not-so-long and not-quite-distinguished career, I allowed myself the self-satisfying thought that I had finally arrived as a performer.

At the very least, I had an affinity for the material.

All of which takes me to my all-time favorite Disney joke—another miscommunication, if you ask me. Here again, the joke is not original to me, but if you repeat it to yourself out loud, in your best impression of Iago the Parrot, I believe I can take some credit for it:

> *A psychiatrist is consulting with Mickey Mouse, after examining Minnie.*
>
> *The doctor says, "Well, Mickey. I've examined Minnie thoroughly, and I'm afraid she's not crazy, as you have described."*

To which Mickey says, "No, doc. You've
misunderstood. I didn't say she was crazy.
I said she was fucking Goofy!"

My fantasy is to record that joke during my next ADR session, and have it somehow turn up in Iago's voice at the Tiki
Room at the Magic Kingdom. (Now, *that's* entertainment,
kids.) But, alas, it's just a fantasy, and as I have demonstrated
time and time again over the years, my fantasies have a way
of bouncing around in my head, over and over, never bursting forth in any sort of meaningful way, although sometimes
there are a few small jets of the stuff that I have to wipe away
with some tissues.

Happily, my calling as a voice-over artist did not end with
this wisecracking parrot. I even moved up in the cartoon
world and started doing voices for actual human characters. I
appeared a few times in the animated series, *Clerks,* which was
based on the Kevin Smith movie of the same name. It was like
an indie-cartoon, which meant that it was smart and subtle
and that nobody really watched it. In any case, for a few moments, in a small, meaningless way, I was pretty damn hip.
Kevin Smith and his partners got a bunch of celebrities to do
cameo appearances as themselves, and when certain celebrities were unavailable or unwilling to stoop to lending their
voices to a hardly seen indie-cartoon, they looked to me. For
example, they wrote a couple lines for Jerry Seinfeld, but
he refused to read them, so the producers got together and
thought who they might know who could do an annoying
Jerry Seinfeld impression. I was their man—and I nailed it.

I even did a bit on *Clerks* as Patrick Swayze, only nobody

really knew what Patrick Swayze sounded like. They knew he danced nicely and looked good in a leotard, so when they asked me to play him in an episode I didn't worry too much about my impression. I just read the lines as myself, which worked out fairly well because nobody really knew what I sounded like, either. As long as the character was well drawn, I was ahead of the game. And just to be on the safe side, I wore my very best leotard to the studio that day. In my mind, at least, I *was* Patrick Swayze. Nobody could tell me any different. And nobody puts this baby in the corner.

It was such a tragedy when Patrick Swayze died—so young, so soon. But the real tragedy, which went unreported in most of the obituaries I read after his death, was that it now appeared they'd never show this *Clerks* episode again. And it was such a shame, too, because I'd done some of my best work on that episode.

Somewhere along the way, I had an opportunity to lend my vocal talents to another wisecracking winged creature. Careful readers will note here that I keep using words like *artist* and *talents* to describe my role or my abilities—but be assured, I do not overstate. There is indeed an art to providing just the right nuance in these sorts of voice-over roles. It is indeed a talent. I know this because this is what I keep telling myself. Before my next career-defining turn, however, I lent my vocal talents to several lesser roles. I played a mechanical bird in a cartoon series called *Cyberchase*. I did the voice of an ant in an insecticide commercial, and the voice of a toaster in a Pop-Tarts commercial. As you can see, I showed a lot of range. And speaking of range, I was once offered the part of a far more major appliance—a gas range, in fact—only I had to turn it down because it felt like too much of a reach. Plus, my gas range had been somewhat handi-capped by that childhood poison-sumac-in-my-sphincter in-cident, so the producers looked to Robert Mitchum instead.

But my voice-over work didn't become truly iconic until some advertising agency contacted my agent and asked if I could play the part of a talking duck in a commercial for an insurance company. It sounded like the stupidest campaign in the history of television. Plus, I'd never even heard of the insurance company—which, it turned out, only offered *supplemental* insurance. My agent mentioned this to me as if I'd have the first fucking clue what the hell he was talking about.

Still, I was a struggling actor, so I heard him out. Then I asked an important question, the answer to which would have a lot to do with my motivation as a character, and my deci-sion to consider the role. I said, "How much does it pay?"

The commercial was for a company called Aflac. Like I said, I'd never heard of it—but then, I was just becoming fa-miliar with companies like Nike and Xerox and Coca-Cola, because I'm slow to grasp developing trends. For all my en-tertainment industry insight and savvy, I don't exactly have a nose for fads and phenomena. Still, I had to go in and read for the role, even though the "role" was just one word. I always tell people it came down to me and Liam Neeson, and if things had gone another way it could have been Liam Neeson shouting out "Aflac!" in an annoying voice, pretending to be a duck, and me starring in *Schindler's List,* merely emoting in an annoying voice, pretending to be a righteous Gentile.

The idea for the Aflac commercial was that this duck would waddle into all these different scenes, interrupting all these different people wondering where to turn for supplemental insurance. It's the kind of thing that happens every day, in small towns all across this great land, right? They weren't very bright, these characters in the commercials. They'd turn around and face the duck, who kept shouting out "Aflac!" in response to their wondering, but they could never quite put two-and-two together. Either they were hard-of-hearing or hard-of-listening or just plain fucking clueless. It must have been very frustrating for the duck—that is, if it had been a real duck, and if it had been able to talk, and if it had actually been trying to be helpful.

I got the part, but it was a struggle. I could never remember my line. Yes, I know, it was only one word, which I was supposed to deliver with a loud, honking, quacklike voice, but as I have indicated I'm something of a perfectionist. When you work with an accomplished actor like Gilbert Gottfried, everything has to be *just so*. And so, just to be on the safe side, I kept throwing up my hands in confusion and despair and turning to the script girl and asking, "Line?"

I never thought it would amount to anything, this little commercial gig. It was a booking, that's all, something for me to do between summer stock performances of Shakespeare. Even Mr. Aflac wondered what the hell he was doing, spending all that money he'd earned from his clients' supplemental insurance premiums on such a silly campaign. But the commercials were a big hit. Right after the first one started airing, in 2000, people all over the country started waddling up to perfect strangers—in their local barbershops, their town squares, their mom-and-pop markets—just waiting for someone to ask an innocent question about supplemental insurance, at which point they'd shout, "Aflac!" They'd storm their friends and neighbors by surprise. Usually, this happened to great merriment and good cheer, although occasionally the person doing the shouting would do so in such a startling manner that people were dropping dead from heart attacks—in a sidelong way, reinforcing the need for a good supplemental insurance plan.

Very quickly, we went back to the studio to record another bunch of spots for the same campaign. Weirdly, perhaps even frighteningly, the ad agency people had me come in and read the line all over again, each time out. I never understood why they couldn't just use the same recording from the first session, but I never questioned it. I was getting paid, and I had to think these people knew what they were doing. That, or maybe they just figured that as long as they were paying me they might as well bust my balls and make me come in to the studio, but I choose to give them the benefit of the doubt on this. Maybe, just maybe they were looking for some subtle differences in my performances, each time I delivered my line. Maybe, just maybe there was a group of earnest-seeming ad-agency-types, carefully logging each and every take, making meticulous little notes on their yellow legal pads to remind them which readings might work best in each of their different scripted scenarios.

"I think the duck sounds so sweet and vulnerable in Take 612," one of the Aflac ad guys might have said. "Let's go with that one."

"Oh, but Take 1,343 is so much funnier," another ad guy might have said. "Gilbert was really feeling it that day."

And on and on.

Now here we are, ten years and probably a million takes later, and they're still making those Aflac commercials. They're still calling me in, asking me to reread my line, and each time I try to bring something new to my interpretation because, as I have written, I'm a real professional. (Also, as I have written, they continue to pay me, and I wasn't raised to accept handouts.) I'm always careful when I talk about that campaign, not to make too much fun of it, or to criticize the good people behind it, or to look such a transparent gift duck in the mouth in any way, because I know it's only a matter of time before someone at the ad agency will look up from his sheaf of yellow legal pages and say, "Wait a minute, screw Gilbert, we can just get an actual duck for this."

Curiously, they even ran this campaign in Japan, but over there they found my voice too abrasive. These are people who have had their villages attacked by Godzilla, so that's saying something, that I come across as too abrasive. It always reminds me how you sometimes hear two people arguing, and one of them says, "Well, I can't speak for the Japanese." In my case, I *legally* can't speak for the Japanese.

One of the great side benefits to being involved in such a long-running campaign is the way it's brought my work to the attention of some of the hottest young starlets in show business. That duck is like catnip to beautiful women, I've learned. For a long time, I was told, Jennifer Lopez used to shout out, "Aflac!" whenever she had sex. I could only assume that she was so drawn to my work that she dreamed constantly of fucking me, even as she was fucking someone else.

After that, my sources told me, Jennifer Garner started doing the same thing. She'd make love to her husband and scream, "Aflac!" Thinking of me, of course—just one of the many burdens of the vast and intimidating nature of my celebrity, and the depth of my fully realized performance. I was only too happy to take one for the Aflac team in this regard.

Another great benefit was the chance to make advertising history. Or, at least, to make the single worst entrance in advertising history. Not too long ago, the Aflac duck was inducted into the Advertising Hall of Fame, along with dozens of other popular commercial characters. Speedy, the Alka-Seltzer tablet. Tony the Tiger. The California Raisins. Mr. Peanut. The Pillsbury Doughboy—or, Poppin' Fresh, as he is known to his professional colleagues. Snap, Crackle and Pop. All these great characters, going back fifty years, and someone in charge thought to include the Aflac duck, even though we'd only been doing the campaign for about five years at that point.

It was a great honor. I know this because that's what I was told. Anyway, it was an honor. Besides, I'd never been inducted into anything, so I was only too happy to show up for a parade to mark the occasion. I'd never been in a parade, either, so this was shaping up to be a big day for me. It never occurred to me that I might look a little foolish, straddling the backseat of a convertible as it snaked its way up Madison Avenue to the induction ceremony. Even if it did, it would never have occurred to me to mind, because I was used to looking a little foolish. (Foolish and me, we had a history.) Anyway, it wasn't like one of those ticker-tape parades the city throws for the Yankees when they win the World Series. I wasn't riding in any kind of classic car, or sticking my head through the roof of a limousine. I was just sitting uncomfortably on the headrest of some guy's Hyundai convertible, throwing stuffed ducks to the parade-goers we passed on our way. And it's not like the streets were lined with throngs of people. In fact, I don't think I saw a single throng along the entire route. There was more like a smattering of people, every here and there, usually waiting for the light to turn at a crosswalk.

Some of the other characters, representing some of the bigger brands, were paraded around on elaborate floats, but there was no such star treatment for me and the duck. Oh, did I mention that I was joined on the backseat of that Hyundai by a giant inflatable duck? Funny, how that little detail almost escaped my retelling . . . but there he was, soaking up the small sliver of limelight that should have been just for me, flapping in the breeze like one of those low-rent inflatable stick figures you sometimes see on used car lots.

It really was quite a moment, stuck somewhere between a thrill and a humiliation. As a matter of fact, it was the humiliation part that got me into some trouble, because I kept putting my head down, hoping no one would recognize me. When we started out, our car was sandwiched between the Planters Peanut float in front, and the Poppin' Fresh float just behind us, but I looked up from my embarrassment at one point and couldn't spot any trace of a parade. Suddenly, there was a city bus in front of us, and a cab stuck in traffic right behind us, and my idiot driver had somehow taken a bunch of wrong turns and was now inching down Ninth Avenue in bumper-to-bumper traffic. People were looking at me, sitting on the backseat of this cheap convertible, next to a giant stuffed duck, wondering what the fuck I was doing. And the worst part was I was all out of stuffed ducks to throw at people, so it's not like I was armed or able to defend myself.

For the life of me, I couldn't imagine how we had drifted all the way to Ninth Avenue, headed downtown, when we should have been headed uptown on Madison. It's like we were in two different boroughs. By this point, the rest of the Hall of Fame characters had made it to the end of the route, where they were supposed to be honored in a special cere-mony. They had bleachers set up, in case anyone wanted to sit down and watch, and a podium so some hot-shit executive could make a speech, but no one could figure out what had happened to me and the duck, and the people in charge didn't want to begin their presentation until I arrived on the scene.

Snap and Pop were particularly put out by the delay, I was later told. Crackle, it turned out, was struggling through the first steps of a 12-step program for saccharine addiction, so he had to drop from the route at some point with an artifi-cially induced case of sugar shock. But every other character had made it to the ceremony. Every other character made an appropriate, timely entrance. Even the M&M boys were on hand, refusing to melt in the heat of what was turning out to be a tense professional moment.

(I heard that and thought, Good for them. They're regular troupers, those M&M boys . . .)

In the end, it took almost two hours for my idiot driver to finally get me and the duck to the closing ceremony, after giv-ing me a tour of Manhattan I didn't particularly need, and the whole way over I kept thinking of ways to explain our disap-pearance. In my defense, I was in character, and ducks are not known for their sense of direction, so I decided to go with that.

Clip 'n' Save Joke no. 8 ✄

A man is stranded on a deserted island with supermodel Cindy Crawford. Every day, he tries to have sex with her, but she keeps pushing him away. After several weeks, the man breaks down and pleads with her. He says, "Look, I'm going crazy on this island, staring at you walking around. I desperately need to have sex with you. No one is going to see us, since we're all alone here. And, most likely, we will never be discovered on this island, so no one will ever know. So please, I beg you. Just do this for me."

Cindy Crawford considers this for a long moment and finally says, "Okay."

So the man and the supermodel have sex, and they're lying in the sand afterward. The man turns to Cindy Crawford and says, "Can you do one more thing for me?"

Cindy Crawford looks at him in an exasperated way and says, "What is it this time?"

The man says, "Would you please dress up as a man?"

Cindy Crawford considers this for another long moment and finally says, "Okay."

The man then gives the supermodel some of his clothes. Cindy Crawford puts on a suit, a shirt, and a tie. The man looks her over and draws a mustache over her lip with a fountain pen, and then he brushes her hair back in a man's style.

Soon, Cindy Crawford is standing next to the man, looking very much like a man herself, wearing a suit, a shirt, and a tie, with a mustache and a man's hairstyle.

Seeing her like this, the man nudges the supermodel in the ribs, slaps her on the back and says proudly, "I just fucked Cindy Crawford."

8

Gag Reflex

Originally, the title of this chapter was going to be the title of the whole book, but then I went away to one of those writer's retreats and came up with the title *Rubber Balls and Liquor,* which I liked a lot better.

However, that left me with the problem of what to do with my original title. I hated to see it go to waste, so I decided to use it as a chapter title instead. But that only created another problem, because it had nothing to do with any of the chapters I planned to write, even though it's the only title I could think of that has something to do with eating disorders, blow jobs and offensive comedy—three things I especially enjoy. Other than *Gone with the Wind,* of course, but that one's already taken.

I suppose I could have come up with an entirely new chapter, one I hadn't planned to write, but that would have meant more work for me so I figured I would just use the title. It doesn't mean anything. It doesn't go with anything. But I went to all that trouble coming up with it.

Now, before you go telling your friends and relations that Gilbert Gottfried is a lazy, no-account Jew who can't be bothered to write fresh, new material on every page of his side-splittingly hilarious and thought-provoking new book, hear me out. And, don't be so quick to judge. I sincerely meant to write an entire chapter, to go along with my achingly clever chapter title, but I had a previous commitment. I'm a busy man. At least I give the appearance of being busy, which is close enough to the same thing. No, I'm not busy like James Brown, who for the longest time was known as the hardest-working man in show business. Certainly, he's slowed down a bit since his death, but he's got a long way to go before he slows all the way down to my level. Me, I like to think I'm the hardliest-working man in show business. It's what I aspire to. As a matter of fact, I'm thinking of trademarking the phrase, and putting it on T-shirts, and possibly developing it into a theme song or maybe even a line of adult diapers, but I'm afraid this would require too much effort and possibly contradict the nickname.

And yet despite my lackluster work ethic I sometimes have a conflict on my schedule, which appears to be the case here with this nonchapter. I won't trouble you with the details of this conflict, because it's probably better if you don't know. Suffice it to say that it involves lunch meat. And caulk.

So what do you say we just sit back and enjoy this clever title, shall we?

Clip 'n' Save Joke no. 9 ✂-----------

A Jewish man is stranded on a deserted island. After being there for a few days, he builds himself a shack. He keeps adding to it and adding to it, until he looks up one day and realizes he has built a beautiful three-bedroom house. He then proceeds to put in some nice landscaping. Somehow, he grows a nice patch of grass, and adds some benches to make a small park.

A few months pass and a ship lands on the island. The captain of the ship sees that the old Jewish man has not only built a beautiful three-bedroom house, with lovely parklike surroundings, but also a museum, a synagogue, a school, a firehouse, another synagogue and a police station. The captain is amazed at this entire village that the old Jew has built, and he says, "This is remarkable. My only question to you is why are there two synagogues?"

The old Jew considers the question for a moment and makes a sour face. Then he points to one of the synagogues disgustedly and says, "You see that one over there? I never go to that one."

9

Circle Gets the Square

I watched a lot of television as a kid. We've covered that, but I want to emphasize the point. In all fairness to me—and it's my book, so from this point on *all fairness to me* should just be assumed—it's not like I could have put my time to more productive use on the Internet. I couldn't play Pong or do a Rubik's Cube, because those things hadn't been invented yet. I couldn't run for office or start a movement, because I preferred my pursuits to be a lot more trivial. I suppose I could have hung out with my friends, but I didn't have any, so that pretty much left television.

You have to realize, I wasn't exactly like the other kids in the neighborhood, or even the other kids in my family. (Well, you don't *have* to come to this realization, but I believe it helps.) I couldn't study to be a doctor or a lawyer. It's not like I had any interests, beyond movie monsters and jerking off. What was my poor mother supposed to say each afternoon when I came home from school?

Gilbert, try jerking off to Betty once in a while! That Veronica gets all the attention!

Gilbert, go to your room and study to be a filthy, degenerate, moderately successful comedian!

She couldn't even send me to my room, because I didn't have one. It was a small apartment, so I slept in the living room, which worked out well because that's where we kept the television. Lucky for me, it was the golden age of afternoon television. There were *Superman* reruns, and game shows like *Password* and *What's My Line?* where you'd see celebrities who were famous for being on game shows. Hey, it was New York City, the throbbing, pulsing center of the media, and anytime you get to use words like *throbbing* and *pulsing* to describe whatever it is you're in the center of, it's probably a good place to be. Even if you're just off to the side, where I usually liked to stand, chances are it's not so bad. Throbbing and pulsing media center or not, we only had a few channels, but there was plenty to watch, believe me.

One of my favorite shows was *Hollywood Squares,* which in those days was hosted by a guy named Peter Marshall, and featured moderately successful comedians like Paul Lynde, Rose Marie, and Charley Weaver. Also, Charo. It's hard not to love a program that offered an exciting young talent like Charo an opportunity to demonstrate her many and varied gifts as an entertainer.

She was particularly adept at rolling her *r*'s, as I recall.

It's good to have something to shoot for, so here I collected these marginal celebrity-types and moderately successful comedians like role models of the entertainment industry. I'd watch and think, *That could be me someday.*

Or, *Who needs medical school?*

Or, *Wally Cox! Wow! To do voices for cartoon animals! Jeepers, it doesn't get any better than this!*

But then, underneath those hopeful considerations, there would be a darker, more sinister line of thought. I'd think, *Boy, how pathetic do you have to be to be on* Hollywood Squares*?*

Even at twelve or thirteen years old, I was pretty jaded, I guess.

Okay, so that's the setup to a *Hollywood Squares* story I'm determined to share. For my money, there's nothing like a good *Hollywood Squares* story to put a real shine to a Hollywood memoir. In George Gobel's book, readers might remember, there was a rollicking good story about *Hollywood Squares* and a surplus case of Lemon Pledge that people are still talking about. (What they're saying, exactly, I couldn't exactly say.) In *her* book, the loud-mouthed comedienne Kaye Ballard wrote wistfully about a tragic incident, involving an unintended use of one of the show's oversized *X*'s from the prop department. (Also, in a sidelong way, she referenced an unnamed "lover" who came to her "square" when a sudden power "surge" darkened the *Hollywood Squares* set during a taping, who was believed to be famed song-and-dance-and-windswept-hair man John Davidson.) And who can forget the stirring account from Orson Welles about the time the show's producers asked him ever-so-carefully if he'd mind occupying one of the ground-floor squares, in consideration of the few extra pounds of winter weight he appeared to be carrying?

Without further ado, then, my *Hollywood Squares* story . . .

Oh, wait. I forgot. There's just one more *ado*. Sorry. There's a Henry Winkler anecdote I need to fold into this thing, as a kind of setup, because I plan to come back to it later, as a kind of punch line. I'll begin the anecdote by stating the obvious: Henry Winkler is one of the nicest guys in the entertainment industry. I know this because Henry Winkler told me so himself, in no uncertain terms. He said, "Gilbert, you won't find a nicer guy than me in this town."

Then he said, "I don't know how I could put this in terms that are any more certain."

Regrettably, Henry Winkler said this in the small town of Hoot Owl, Oklahoma, where we were performing in a dinner theater production of *Man of La Mancha,* so I don't know that he was saying all that much. Indeed, the town of Hoot Owl was so small, it couldn't even support a dinner theater. It was more like an appetizer theater, and the portions were not very filling.

To Henry Winkler's credit, though, he said these nice things in the sincere, soft-spoken voice he uses on talk shows, and not in the loud, over-the-top, Fonzie voice that made him famous. Have you ever heard this man talk, in real life? He sounds like he's on antidepressants. When you compare it to how he talks in fake life, as Arthur Fonzarelli, the contrast is startling. And, unsettling.

In all seriousness, or at least in some, Henry Winkler did actually come up to me to introduce himself and say nice things at a comedy awards show. He did speak slowly and softly, like a bad therapist. I don't think we were in Hoot Owl, but I could be wrong. He sought me out backstage, and he took my right hand in both of his in an overly enthusiastic two-fisted greeting that was meant to connote warmth and genuine good feeling.

He said, "Gilbert, what a pleasure it is to watch you on-stage." He said this as if he really, really meant it. More than that, he said it as though he had just watched Christ Himself perform a hilarious five-minute set—from the cross, no less. (Talk about a tough room!) Henry Winkler's famous, prime-time eyes opened up, and his famous, prime-time smile widened, and he went on and on about how I was one of the most amazing comedians he had ever seen. I believe he used the phrase "legendary brilliance," although here again I could be wrong. He could have used the phrase "not half-bad for a filthy, godforsaken Jew," but you can certainly understand how I might confuse the one for the other.

Oh, he was fairly gushing, my new friend and admirer Henry Winkler. In fact, I was a little worried about all this gushing. I thought if he wasn't careful with his gushing he might get a touch of semen on the lapel of my sports jacket, that's how much the Fonz was gushing. He was a regular geyser, this one.

Okay, so that's the Henry Winkler backstory to set up my *Hollywood Squares* front story—and now, finally, I'm all out of *ado*'s.

Cut to a whole bunch of years later, and *Hollywood Squares* was back on the air. It turns out that it's one of those shows that just won't go away, like the news, and this time around Whoopi Goldberg was one of the producers. She was also in the center square, which is a place of extreme honor on the *Hollywood Squares* set. It's like being the headliner, only not so much. You're still sitting in a box, answering stupid questions, and fooling yourself into thinking it's a good gig, only you're doing it from a position of prominence. As a career move, it falls somewhere between earning an Academy Award for *Ghost* and playing Dulcinea in that appetizer theater production of *Man of La Mancha*.

Well, it turns out there is a God and—who would have thought?—He sometimes listens to awkward Jewish boys from Brooklyn who question the wisdom of appearing on afternoon game shows. I know this because at some point Whoopi called and asked if I'd appear on the show. To be accurate, Whoopi didn't make the call herself. She had one of her people do it. My people were busy when the call came in, so I answered it myself. I said, "Sure, I'll appear on *Hollywood Squares*. What the hell."

(Beneath the category of "Be Careful What You Wish For" moments that find us over the course of a lifetime, there is a subcategory known as "Be Careful What You Disdain," and if you look closely you can find a listing for me under "*Hollywood Squares*: Gottfried, Gilbert; childhood hostility toward . . .")

So I talked to Whoopi's people, and soon after that my people talked to her people, and soon after that I flew out to California to tape a week's worth of shows, and I can only assume it went reasonably well because from time to time afterward the producers would ask me back. I became a real favorite. At least, I became a real favorite of mine. I particularly enjoyed watching myself on that show, and I guess the folks at home did as well, because Whoopi's people kept asking me back.

After one of my first appearances on the show, Whoopi got a phone call to complain about my material. The call was from Hollywood legend Marlon Brando. At first, Whoopi didn't believe it was Hollywood legend Marlon Brando on the other end of the line, but then he did his best Marlon Brando impression and she was convinced. He could be very convincing that way, I'm told. Anyway, it seemed that Hollywood legend Marlon Brando was upset about a joke I'd told earlier that week. The joke, like all jokes on *Hollywood Squares,* came in response to a question.

The question: "What animal has the largest eyes in the world?"

My answer: "Marlon Brando at a buffet."

It was an easy, throwaway line, aimed at an easy, hard-to-miss target, and it must have hit its mark because Hollywood legend Marlon Brando was on the phone to Whoopi Goldberg right after the program aired. He was not amused, Whoopi could tell. In fact, he was offended and angered. He said, "Am I going to be the running joke on your show?"

Of course, he said this in his cartoonish *Godfather* voice, which meant it came out sounding like a hoarse-whisperer with a mouthful of marbles. Whoopi never told me what she said in response, but I like to imagine that she said, "Running? You? Come on, Marlon. It'd be more like a lumbering joke. Or maybe a slowly-getting-up-out-of-your-chair joke, but running is out of the question." What was she supposed to say? The man was tipping the scales at over five hundred pounds. Blinking his eyes could have given him a heart attack.

I heard about the phone call from another one of the producers, and it made me think. What I thought was this: *Hmmm . . . that seems like a good idea. Thanks for the suggestion, Hollywood legend Marlon Brando.*

And so, from that moment on, I made it a special point to make Marlon Brando into a running joke on *Hollywood Squares*.

Some examples . . .

The question: "The largest boom in recorded history came from Krakatoa. What was Krakatoa?"

My answer: "Japan's first Mexican restaurant. And do you know who was eating there? Marlon Brando."

The question: "The alien grows bigger and bigger as it consumes everything in its path. Steve McQueen stars in it. What's the film?"

My answer: "The Marlon Brando Story."

To which Whoopi weighed in to defend her legendary friend. She got all up in my grille and said in her funny, street-smart way, "Leave Marlon alone."

To which I weighed in to defend myself. I got right back up in her grille and said in my own funny, street-smart way, "I was gonna say, 'The Dustin Hoffman Story,' but then I remembered he doesn't weigh seven thousand pounds."

Oh, I could go on and on. And, much to the dismay of Hollywood legend Marlon Brando, I did.

My very favorite *Hollywood Squares* joke? Well, I thought you'd never ask . . .

The question: "In a woman's magazine, which television show did women say accurately portrays the single girl, *Sex and the City* or *Ally McBeal*?"

"Okay, I know this one," I started in.

"Why?" came the response, from Whoopi and the others, who knew at some point to question my authority.

"Because," I explained, "I go clothes shopping with Calista

Flockhart, and every time she puts on a new outfit she goes, 'Does this dress make my spinal cord look big?'"

(Oh, I guess I should mention here that I also specialized in Calista Flockhart jokes, but that's for another book.)

(Also, with the way I treated Harrison Ford in a previous chapter, I can't imagine the Ford-Flockharts will be giving this book as a Christmas gift this year—or any other year, for that matter—so if you happen to receive this book from Harrison or Calista by mistake, please be kind enough to exchange it for something more flattering to the lovely couple.)

It was during Whoopi's run as one of the show's producers that I found myself in the middle of one of the great comic moments in game show history. Understand, the phrase *one of the great comic moments in game show history* is somewhat loaded, because I believe there was just this one moment. Personally, I don't count the time that accountant from Des Moines and his farm-fed wife dressed up as two steaming piles of shit on *Let's Make a Deal,* because that's physical humor, and I don't believe you can equate a pratfall or a steaming pile of shit with subtle wordplay or witty banter or legendary brilliance.

I'll admit, it's disingenuous to suggest that I was in the middle of this great comic moment, because here again, I was off to the side. Let's be clear: Whoopi was in the middle, in the center square. That's where all the action was on that show—which, after all, was *her* show. Me, I was in the upper-right corner of the famous *Hollywood Squares* board, which I remember thinking at the time was a pretty good metaphor for my career, working in the margins of a marginal game show. I used to think that if the *Hollywood Squares* producers believed they could have added another row of squares, and assigned me to my rightful spot even farther from the action without somehow altering the rules of the universally beloved childhood game of tic-tac-toe, it would have more accurately reflected my role.

So there I was, not quite front and center but rather tucked into the corner, as far away from the action as possible, when the poor contestant had no choice but to throw the question to me. The way the show works, for those of you who have been too busy or too full of yourselves these past few decades to watch afternoon television, is there are nine so-called celebrities, seated in nine different spots on a giant tic-tac-toe board.

(For those of you who are just too stupid to know the rules of tic-tac-toe, you should probably think about reading a book with a few less words in it.)

Back to the game: there are two contestants, representing an X and an O—just like the game itself!—and they take turns asking the celebrities all these different questions. They don't actually come right out and ask the questions themselves; there's a Peter Marshall–like game show host who does it for them. Some of the questions are no-brainers, and some of them are graduate school level—that is, if there was a graduate school for obscure bits of useless information. The celebrity usually makes a lame joke, which is very often prepared for them by the show's writers, and then offers a best guess for an answer. Then it's up to the contestant to decide if he or she agrees with the celebrity, and if they get it right they put their X or their O in the square. If they get it wrong, the opponent puts *their* mark in the square. The first contestant to collect three squares in a row is the winner, and gets a motorboat or a wall of E-ZBrick paneling for their family room or a sun-soaked, fun-filled dream vacation for two to Branson, Missouri, or some other fabulous prize chosen especially for them.

Got it?

Good—except there's one wrinkle. (Curses! There's always a wrinkle!) If a player needs a square to make three in a row, he must answer the question directly in order to do so. What that means is you can't just sit back and hope the other guy screws up, like you have for the rest of the game. You actually have to do something to win the fabulous prize.

Joining me on the show that week were big stars and not-so-big stars and stars who were only big in their own minds. There was Whoopi, in her usual spot in the center square. There was Jason Alexander, from *Seinfeld*. There was Little Richard. There were Penn & Teller, sharing the same square, which always struck me as a little bit gay and insulting, to have to fit into such a tight space and share such a narrow cone of spotlight with someone else, even if you were partners in a comedy-magic duo. There were two actresses from the sitcom *Dharma & Greg*, neither of which played Dharma or Greg. And there were two other comics, Judy Gold and Bruce Vilanch. And then there was me, in the upper-right-hand corner of the board. Not exactly the most star-studded group of celebrities to ever grace a Hollywood soundstage, but we were all variously happy to be there.

Well, it came to pass that my colleagues were no help at all to the two contestants on the show that day. It also came to pass that I found myself in a situation where I could use a phrase like *it came to pass* and have it sound like I was writing a bad detective novel. Me and my celebrity pals were playing for a guy named David, a police officer from Los Angeles, in the *X* spot, and a woman named Valerie, a librarian from Texas, who (oddly) introduced herself as a wedding and funeral singer, in the *O* spot. The contestants went back and forth, deep into the game. They went all the way through our tic-tac-toe board until they had no choice but to look to me, because by that point I was the only schmuck left on the board, which was now set up in such a way that I couldn't help David make a run of three *X*'s or Valerie make a run of three *O*'s. All I could do was help one of them earn the final square—which according to the rules of the game show would have been just enough to win.

The question: "*Playgirl* magazine's clinical sexologist says, 'I think we should be able to talk about sex the way we talk about' . . . what?"

My answer: "Soft-boiled eggs, because they both take under three minutes."

This wasn't a particularly funny answer, I'll admit, but I went with my gut. The audience laughed anyway, because I've learned that television game show audiences will laugh at almost anything, except here their howls of laughter only made me feel cheap and unworthy, so I followed up my first response with another. I said, "I know this one, because I posed for *Playgirl*. You don't actually see anything, because my thumb was in the way."

This time, it felt to me as if the laughter was deserved.

Finally, I gave my answer: "Food."

David, the cop, disagreed with me, but I tried not to take it personally.

I was right, of course.

(I usually was.)

And he was wrong.

(They usually were, when they disagreed with me.)

Penn Jillette took the opportunity to tell David the cop what he thought of his game-playing skills—and, relatedly, his decision to disagree with a great thinker and well-known sexology expert like Gilbert Gottfried.

He shouted, "You fool!"

Then, the studio audience howled with studio audience laughter, which apparently is what studio audiences do when an oversized magician yells at one of the contestants onstage.

(You had to be there, I guess.)

Then, Valerie the singing librarian called on me to help her with the next question. Who the hell else was she supposed to call on? All of the other squares were completed. Technically, all of the other celebrity panelists were off the clock. We could have sent them out for coffee, but I needed them to hang around and laugh at my jokes.

The question: "In a poll, 94 percent of Hungarians, compared to only 46 percent of Americans, said doing this was necessary in order to feel fulfilled. Doing what?"

I thought, *Who comes up with these questions?* And, *Could they make this game any more convoluted or complicated?*

My answer: "Seeing Wayne Newton, live."

Again, not the funniest answer in the history of American comedy, or even in the history of Hungarian comedy, but you'd never know it from the howling fits of laughter that burst from the studio audience—a good deal of which had not been prerecorded.

My real answer: "Having a child."

Valerie, a woman who actually made a chunk of her living singing at funerals, disagreed—a fool move that was right up there with trying to get booked at a graveside gig.

And I said as much. I followed Penn's lead and yelled out, "You fool!"

This in turn got another big response from the audience, and from the other celebrities, who were by now wondering when it might be their turn again. But they'd have to wait a while, because David and Valerie were unwilling to trust that I might actually know what I was talking about. They kept throwing to me, because of course they had no choice, and I kept answering the question correctly, in a mildly amusing way, and they kept disagreeing with me. Or, I'd offer up some ridiculous answer that couldn't possibly be true, and then they'd go and agree with me. We were getting nowhere. Then we'd break for commercial, and come back and continue on our way. Six or seven times, we went back and forth in this way, and each time I'd shout down to David or Valerie, "You fool!"—each time, to wild fits of hysterical and suspicious laughter, a good deal of which had not been prerecorded.

Finally, after we'd all had just about enough, I correctly suggested that the word *smog* comes from a combination of the words *smoke* and *fog*, and Officer Dave very smartly agreed with me . . . putting us all out of our misery.

It was, we were told, the single longest game in tic-tac-toe history—that is, if the producers of *Hollywood Squares* could even be trusted with tic-tac-toe history. All these years later, I still get stopped by people in airports who pull me aside and shout, "You fool!" Naturally, I assume they're referring to this interminable game of *Hollywood Squares* and to the catchphrase that developed on the back of it, although I suppose it's possible they're just referring to me in general.

And that might have been that, except that it wasn't, because we've reached the point in the story where careful readers are probably asking themselves, "Where the fuck is Fonzie?"

Good question. Remember, I promised to get back to our friend and admirer Henry Winkler before too terribly long, and I think we can all agree that it's been too terribly long enough. What happened was Whoopi Goldberg and her producing partners decided they'd had enough of the *Hollywood Squares* business and announced they'd be leaving the show. It's like they looked up one day and realized, *Hey, this is syndicated afternoon television. What the fuck are we doing?* This worried me, at first, because I'd carved out a nice little niche for myself, on these particular fringes of the entertainment industry, along with a nice little paycheck. I'd come to rely on these things. A little bit of money, a small measure of fame, an endless supply of complimentary beverages delivered directly to my upper-right-hand corner square . . . it all added up, and now I didn't want it to be taken away. Like every other self-centered, semi-celebrity person in show business, I considered the situation in terms of what it meant to me, to my career, to my bank account—and at just that moment it didn't look so hot.

For a couple weeks, I thought seriously of becoming a tire salesman, but then it was announced that the show would be continuing, and that Henry Winkler would be one of the new producers, and I thought, *Ayyyyyy.* I was in. Golden. Good to go.

This guy loved me, I remembered. After all, how could I forget? I still had that cum-stained sports jacket I was wearing when he gushed all over me. I'd called the Smithsonian, so they could put it on display, right next to Fonzie's leather biker jacket, but they hadn't come by to pick it up just yet.

("Whatever you do," the Smithsonian people said, "don't send it out to the cleaners.")

So I set these developments aside, and figured I was all set. With my great and admiring pal Henry Winkler now in charge, a part of me thought they might even change the format and start calling it *Hollywood Square,* and I'd be the entire show.

But then I went to the set the next day and I could tell something was amiss. Or, maybe it was afoot. I can never tell with those two. *Afoot, amiss . . .* something was *off,* let's just say that. The tip-off was that people came up to me and said things like, "We're really going to miss you around here, Gilbert." Call me crazy, but I started to get an uneasy feeling that things weren't going to work out. And, sure enough, they didn't. The new producers wanted to give the show a whole new vibe, a whole new energy—and for some reason, when you think in terms of a whole new vibe, or a whole new energy, there's a tendency to think of anything but me.

To his great credit, I don't believe Henry Winkler was involved in this particular decision. It was his partners, deciding to go this other way. It was nothing personal, they all said. They had this really great idea, they all said. Something no other game show producer had ever thought of before. They wanted to hire only A-list superstars. The new guys got together and thought, *Hey, we've been going about this thing all wrong.* For years and years, they'd booked celebrity guests like Charley Weaver and Jo Anne Worley and Gilbert Gottfried and figured that was good enough, when all along they should have been asking Clark Gable and Jack Nicholson and Meryl Streep. It had just never occurred to them, that's all. So now they were sitting around, trying to freshen up their tired old show, saying, "Let's get Tom Cruise to be the center square."

Or, "What about Julia Roberts, is she still big enough? We'll put her on the 'maybe' list."

And then they'd start making a flurry of phone calls that would never go anywhere and they'd wind up hiring some guy from a toilet paper commercial. It never occurred to them that Robert De Niro might have something better to do. Or that Leonardo DiCaprio felt his name was long enough without adding, ". . . to block."

In the meantime, people at home were writing in, wondering what had happened to Gilbert Gottfried. I wouldn't exactly call it a groundswell, but it was certainly swell. Out there in the heartland, where people actually watch this stuff, I'd struck some sort of chord. It turned out that television audiences actually liked me up there, in the upper-right-hand corner, cracking mildly amusing jokes in a slightly offensive manner. At the very least, they noticed that I was gone, which was something. (It wasn't a lot, mind you, but it was something.) And yet for a long, long time, I never heard from my pal Henry Winkler on this. Well, this wasn't entirely true. Every once in a while, I'd pick up the phone and hear someone say, "Ayyyyyy!" and then hang up, and I could only assume it was Fonzie, letting me know in his own way that even he couldn't rescue me from the vast wasteland of washed-up television game show stars.

But that's Hollywood for you, right? At least, that's Hollywood for *me*.

Clip 'n' Save Joke no. 10 ✂----------------

A truck driver is having his lunch at the counter of a roadside diner. Two Hell's Angels walk in and approach the counter alongside him, looking for trouble. One of the bikers says, "Hey, Fatso." But the truck driver doesn't say anything and tries to continue eating his lunch in peace.

Next, the other Hell's Angel grabs the trucker's sandwich, and throws it down on the ground, and stamps his foot on it. The truck driver still keeps quiet and tries to drink his coffee.

At this, the two Hell's Angels pull the hot cup of coffee from the trucker's hand and dump it on his head. In response, the trucker simply stands, brushes himself off, quietly pays his check, and leaves.

After he walks out, one of the Hell's Angels says, "Boy, that trucker ain't much of a man."

To which the waitress says, "He ain't much of a trucker, either. He just ran over two motorcycles."

10

Celebrity Depth Chart

I'm a firm believer in fame and fortune—mostly, mine. Tell me how much money you have in the bank, or how famous you are, and I'll tune right out, but take an interest in how well *I'm* doing and we can be friends for life. Or at least for the time being.

It's interesting to me that these two markers of success often go hand in hand. I can understand this, because one has quite a lot to do with the other, but on the other hand in hand that's not always the case. You can be world-famous and poor as dirt. Or, you can be one of the richest people on the planet and nobody has heard of you except the people you pay to mismanage your money or give you unnecessary career advice.

The fortune part of being successful is not terribly interesting, because you can measure it, so long as it doesn't involve too many offshore investments. You can attach a number to it and right away you know where you stand. There's nothing to interpret or take into account because it's all right there. The fame part, however, leaves a little something to the imagination or to your own inflated sense of importance. This is especially interesting in the weirdly self-indulgent world of celebrity where I happen to live—a place where those of us who have deliberately set out in search of fame are constantly measuring where we stand in relation to every other person who ever wanted to be famous.

Or maybe it's just me, doing all this measuring. Yeah, I suppose it's possible that I'm the only pathetic loser in the loosely affiliated club of celebrity who keeps running tabs on his place in the pop cultural firmament. Personally, I don't believe that this is the case, but I must allow that such a thing is possible if I hope to come across in these pages with anything resembling credibility.

(And speaking of credibility, I'm told that if you stand back and look at things in just the right way, and if you catch these aspects of character in just the right light, credibility in this regard has been known to resemble envy, but keep in mind I have no personal experience in this area. It's just what I've been told.)

It is, however, an absolute truth that with each rung on the ladder of celebrity we climb past another pathetic loser on his or her way up or down. Line us all up and take us all in, all at once, and by some measure or other we celebrities and semi-celebrities and *wannabe* celebrities will be slightly more or somewhat more or substantially more famous than the person on the adjacent rung—or, slightly less or somewhat less or substantially less famous, as the case may be. (Which, in my case, is very often the case, as the case may be.)

And so, since my credibility has been lightly tossed into question—and here I might have used the word *thrown* in place of this light tossing, except I've never been particularly good at sports and I've been told I throw like a girl—I feel compelled to let you readers in on a little secret: there's a list. Yep, it's true. We keep score. Just to be clear: you didn't hear it from me, but there is definitely a list. I'm not at liberty to say where this list is kept, or who is charged with keeping it, but you'll have to trust me on this—me, and the editors of *Us* magazine, but that's as much as I'm going to say.

Rest assured, we celebrities know where we stand, at all times. We always know which pathetic loser is just above us, and which pathetic loser is just below, and what we have to do to improve our position on the leader board. For one of us to rise, another must fall.

Consider: as of this writing, I am looking directly up the skirt of Lauren Tewes, the hardly remembered actress who is perhaps best hardly remembered for her role as Julie McCoy, the cruise director on TV's *The Love Boat*. If you're keeping score, Lauren Tewes is resting on rung #1,163, while I'm perched somewhat halfheartedly on rung #1,164. Just below me, at #1,165, is Florence Stanley, the gravelly-voiced actress who is perhaps best hardly remembered for playing Abe Vigoda's wife on TV's *Fish*.

(Careful readers will note that Florence Stanley has been dead since 2003, but in my defense for being just barely ahead of a dead sitcom actress let me point out that Florence Stanley lives on in reruns, and in the hearts and minds of devoted *Fish* viewers. Also, without really realizing it, I seem to have played a role in improving her standing by referring to her in a throwaway aside during a previous chapter—and by *throwaway* I of course mean *lightly tossed*. Before that ill-advised reference, which I'm trying to cut in editing, poor

Florence was all the way down at #2,713, which just goes to show you the power of a *lightly tossed-off* aside in a minor work of semi-celebrity nonfiction.)

(Confused readers will wonder just how it is they're supposed to pronounce Lauren Tewes's name, and just how it is that a guy like me can be marginally less famous than someone whose name you can't even pronounce. But that's the sheer genius of Lauren Tewes's celebrity, if you must know. You're not supposed to say her name out loud. Legend has it that something bad happens in Bangladesh, or quite possibly Piscataway, whenever someone tries to speak her name. That's the elusive power of Lauren Tewes and her particular brand of celebrity. We dare not give it voice. We merely acknowledge it, and admire her body of work, and move on.)

My current position on the celebrity ladder presents another one of those delicious ironies I wrote about earlier, because *The Love Boat* itself served as a kind of barometer of fame. If you were on your way up the celebrity ladder, but not yet high enough to have any sort of name recognition or public following, the producers would never have considered you for a guest-starring role. If you were so high up on that celebrity ladder that when you looked down at us little people we appeared through your rose-colored glasses as specks or ants or squirming bits of sperm as they might seem through a microscope, then you would have never considered the producers' requests for you to sign on for a guest-starring role. You needed to be in just the right spot, at just the right time, in order to win a coveted trip aboard the *Pacific Princess*—kind of like being just famous enough to accept an invitation to appear on *Hollywood Squares,* only with motion sickness and a lovely, all-you-can-eat buffet.

Here I am, staring right up Lauren Tewes's skirt—and from the looks of things it's no wonder she hasn't worked all that much in the intervening decades, considering the disinterest she seems to take in the area of personal grooming.

Most times, you know exactly where you stand on the celebrity ladder, but it can get confusing. I like to think I have a good handle on how famous I am at any given moment, but sometimes I'm a little off. One afternoon, I was walking around Manhattan, on lower Broadway, feeling quite full of myself. This doesn't mean I'd just come from a nice lunch, just that I was feeling content with myself and my semi-celebrity existence. My career was going well. Nobody had sued me in quite some time. The chafing around the base of my penis that seems to represent a chronic condition was in a kind of remission. All was right in my peculiar corner of the world—and then, just as I was feeling particularly content, I walked by a group of paparazzi. All of a sudden, my cheerful afternoon took a dark, distasteful turn.

Don't you just hate when that happens? Well, when you're a major semi-celebrity, as I am, you react in a number of different ways to such an intrusion on your privacy. First, you feel a little scared. You can't help yourself. It's like you're being attacked, and you have to gather your wits (which, inexplicably, had just fallen to the sidewalk, like so many loose marbles). You go into survival mode—but when you walk about in the fine sliver of limelight that illuminates your days and the days of all those who cross your path, you get used to this sort of thing. You adjust. You cope.

Second, you become angry. You get your back up. You snarl your teeth a bit, and allow yourself the small, self-satisfying thought that you should perhaps resent this intrusion on your privacy. You lose a little piece of yourself.

And finally, you reach a place of acceptance. You embrace your role in the strange dance of semi-celebrity, and you go with it because there's nothing more you can do. It's the contract you signed the moment you sought fame and fortune on the world's stage—and the agreement seems to be binding even if things don't quite work out, and you haven't managed to become as rich or famous as you'd hoped.

So that's where I was, in this place of acceptance, trying to think how I might renegotiate my semi-celebrity fame contract, when out of nowhere this group of paparazzi seemed to rush toward me, cameras pointing. And do you know what? I was no longer scared, at this point. I was no longer angry. I was numb to those emotions—beaten down by them, really, and now simply willing to play my part. I steeled myself for whatever would happen next, and if you haven't steeled yourself in a while let me assure you it's not always the most pleasant experience. However, just as I prepared my best, camera-ready smile, the photographers shot right past me, like a pack of wolves in search of better, more interesting prey. And as I turned, I could see where they were headed . . . straight for hotshot young actor Liev Schreiber!

I thought, *What the hell is he doing here?*

Apparently, hotshot young actor Liev Schreiber had climbed right past me on that ladder of fame. I should have known, because the celebrity list is updated on a daily basis, usually at the close of show business each evening (Pacific time), but I guess I wasn't paying attention. Conveniently, there's an archive. Go back a few years and you'll find me at #1,994, just ahead of a guy named Victor Willis, the cop from the Village People, and just below Donny Most, from TV's *Happy Days*. If you must know, I was ahead of Ralph Malph for most of my time in show business, but then he started calling himself "Donald" and his career took off—and as he passed me I thought, *All credit to you, my good man.*

(After that, I wished him *Godspeed*.)

(Then, after that, I wished he would change his name back to "Donny.")

For many years, I didn't know the first thing about this celebrity list, and merely assumed that my occasional rise and fall in popularity had to do with the quality of my work, or the work of my publicist. I couldn't have been more wrong. In fact, there was one curious celebrity exchange from early on in my career that I must now reconsider from an entirely new perspective, now that I know about these daily rankings.

It was back in the early 1990s, although it's possible it took place in the 2000s. In any case, I'm almost certain it happened quite a while ago. Whenever it happened, it happened in Las Vegas—and I'm here to report that it's a myth when they say what happens in Vegas stays in Vegas, because this exchange has stayed with me over the years. I was in town to do a series of stand-up shows, and found myself with an evening to kill before starting my run, so I went to see Wayne Newton. Why? Because I could get free tickets, that's why. And because Wayne and I had once worked together in a movie called *The Adventures of Ford Fairlane*. Most people don't remember that we worked together in that movie, but that's only because most people didn't bother to see it.

And so for these reasons and a few others I don't wish to get into here in such a public setting, I went to see Wayne Newton perform. That's the setup. Now, here's what happened: Wayne Newton mentioned me from the stage. That's pretty much it. It doesn't sound like much of a story, I know, but it struck me as such a classic, old-time show business moment, because of course he didn't just mention me. He *introduced* me. (In classic, old-time show business terms, there's a big difference.) I sat there in the audience, and for a brief moment I felt in some small way what it must have been like to be Sammy Davis, Jr., back in the days when everybody in show business seemed to know each other. I think I even closed my eyes and imagined it—although, in the interest of accuracy, I only closed one eye, because that's what Sammy would have done.

It was a great, great moment in my career, I'll admit. Not quite a highlight, but certainly a light, as I will soon make clear. Allow me to further set the scene: Wayne Newton was pretty much oozing his Vegas-style warmth and insincerity from the stage, introducing war veterans and public officials and a few other show business types who were marginally more and less famous than me. He'd give a little shout-out to each person, and there'd be a tiny wave of recognition or admiration or whatever was appropriate, and then he'd make a grand showing of sending over a bottle of champagne to that person's table, typically to enthusiastic applause.

Then he got around to me. Finally. Or at least I thought he was finally getting around to me, but he took such a long way around that for a beat or two I couldn't be sure. On his way to wherever he was going he said, "Ladies and gentleman, what a great honor it is for me to introduce you to a dear friend of mine. And what a great honor it is for me personally that he took the time from his own busy career to come out and see my show."

At this point, I started to think he might have been talking about me, but only because he'd already introduced just about everybody else in the audience. There was no one left, really. Plus, in all likelihood, management was by now all out of champagne, so even if he was finally getting around to me I'd probably just get a glass of water out of the deal.

Then he motioned to the lighting guy up in the booth. He pointed toward me and said, "Can we get a spotlight please?"

And then, with a wave of Wayne Newton's magic hand, the spotlight shone on my table, so I did what most people do when an impossibly bright light is shined in their eyes. I put my hand against my brow like a salute, and squinted like a Navajo Indian and made a concerted effort to look out at the crowd through the glare.

A highlight, no. A light, yes.

"Gilbert Gottfried, ladies and gentleman," my lifelong pal Wayne Newton declared from the stage, as if he were introducing the Pope. To a roomful of Jews.

To thunderous applause, he introduced me. Well, maybe not *thunderous* applause, but it felt for a moment like it might rain. Then my good show business friend Wayne Newton said a few more nice things about me and went back to his show, and as he snapped his fingers in time to the next song I couldn't help but think, *Hey, what about my fucking champagne?*

It was a reasonable thought, wouldn't you agree? I mean, here he'd just given out a dozen bottles of champagne, to lesser luminaries than me. Some of these people were so far down on the ladder of fame it might as well have been a step stool. I didn't even like champagne. I just wanted what was coming to me, but instead I sat there like an idiot, waving from the narrow cone of spotlight that shone briefly on my table.

A couple songs later, my good friend Wayne Newton motioned for the lighting guy again. He shined the spotlight on my table again. In time to the opening bars of the next song, Wayne Newton said, "Let me tell you something about my good friend Gilbert Gottfried, ladies and gentlemen. You know, when you're a performer, the last thing you want to do on your night off is go out and see a show. That's why it's such an honor to have this man in my audience. He's a comedian. He's a movie star. He's so talented, I hate him."

(This was my good friend Wayne Newton adopting a playful, teasing tone.)

Then he waved his hand again and said, "A round of applause, please, for my good friend, Gilbert Gottfried."

There followed another round of applause, because these Vegas crowds tended to do what they were told, and the next thing I knew Wayne Newton was deep into his next song and I was still without my bottle of complimentary champagne.

I was outraged. Well, maybe not outraged, but somewhat put out. Like I said, I didn't particularly care for champagne, but that wasn't the point. The point was it felt to me like I'd been snubbed—relegated to a lower rung than I surely deserved.

Soon, there was another lull in Wayne Newton's between-songs patter, and he asked the lighting guy to seek me out again. This time he said, "And hey, if you don't have plans tomorrow night, go see my good friend Gilbert Gottfried at the House of Blues. And if you do have plans, cancel them."

Still, no champagne—and yet I'd somehow gone from a little put out to a little bit thrilled. Why? Well, this was the sort of inter-celebrity repartee I'd grown up admiring, the kind of back-and-forth that might have passed between Frank Sinatra and one of the lesser Rat Packers. It was all so *inside* and corny, and I loved it and hated it all at the same time. Still, it felt exactly right and good and cool. I could almost forget for a moment that my good friend Wayne Newton was wearing a sequined jumpsuit.

Now, the curious thing about this exchange was the Vegas factor, which must be considered. In Vegas, Wayne Newton is a much bigger deal than he is in the rest of the world. Nothing against my good show business friend Wayne Newton, who is generally considered Las Vegas royalty. In Hollywood, however, he's more like one of the huddled masses. In that theater, on that night, he had me by a couple hundred rungs, easy, but anywhere else we were a pretty even match. Hell, on the *Hollywood Squares* set, I could bring him up as the butt of a corny joke. Anywhere else, he would have sent over that bottle of champagne—which, anywhere else, I would have promptly thrown right back at him, if I didn't happen to throw like a girl.

You never know where you might stand on the depth chart of celebrity, from one day to the next. You can be up one day and down the next, and the day after that you're nowhere. It's harsh and cruel and arbitrary. Some days, you're all these things at once. At some other low point in my career, I found myself on the same famous plane as Marlee Matlin. Sort of. At least, it was a plane.

Perhaps a bit of setup is necessary. Readers will remember Marlee Matlin as the once famous Academy Award–winning deaf actress who eventually found herself typecast as a deaf person. Or maybe they won't, but that's not the point. The point is that I looked a lot like Marlee Matlin's interpreter. Marlee Matlin was so famous after winning her Oscar that she traveled for a brief while with a full-time interpreter, who just happened to look like a short, whiny Jew who told filthy jokes and disrespected women for a living.

And, as much as it pains me to admit, for that same brief while this interpreter fellow was a couple dozen rungs ahead of me on the celebrity ladder, as I recall. Everywhere I went, people would look at me with an odd flash of recognition, and I'd think for a moment that they were trying to place me, from a particularly memorable role in this or that film, but then it would turn out that they had me confused with Marlee Matlin's interpreter. They'd come up to me and say, "Hey, Marlee Matlin's interpreter, could you please tell Marlee she's a silent inspiration to deaf people everywhere?" Or, they'd just flap their hands and make all these foolish gestures and signals as if they were trying to communicate in a secret language based on foolish gestures and hand signals.

On many occasions, Marlee Matlin would show up at an industry event or awards show and someone in charge would come out to greet her and wonder why the hell she'd brought Gilbert Gottfried with her. One talk show host even thought we were dating—which would have been just fine with me, if anyone had thought to ask.

Most young actors, they get their first big breaks in Hollywood and people start confusing them with Robert Redford or Paul Newman. Me, I got confused as Marlee Matlin's interpreter—which would have been helpful in the unlikely event that a casting director ever uttered the phrase, "Quick, get me a Marlee Matlin interpreter–type!"

Okay, so that's the setup. Now, here's the payoff. A couple months into all of this mistaken identity business, I was on a plane to Los Angeles when someone tapped me on the shoulder. (See, I told you there'd be a plane.) I turned around and it was like I was looking in the mirror. It was *him*! Marlee Matlin's interpreter. Apparently, while I'd been going about my days, getting confused for him, he'd been going about his days, getting confused for me. It was a regular two-way street, and now that we had bumped into each other on it he thought he'd introduce himself. Marlee Matlin was sleeping, a couple rows back, so we passed a few pleasant moments chatting and comparing notes. (It turned out he had some of the same difficulties getting laid, which led me to believe it wasn't just *me*, after all . . .) We talked and talked. He was a pretty good guy—and, a good talker. Or maybe he was just so excited to be talking with his mouth that I couldn't shut him up.

After a while, one of us came up with a genius idea. I'd like to take full credit for it, because it really was a genius idea, but I suppose it's possible that Marlee Matlin's interpreter might have had a hand in it—and when you suggest that someone who's fluent in sign language had a hand in giving voice to an idea, that's really saying something.

Anyway, it was decided that I would switch seats with this guy, so I tiptoed back to Marlee Matlin's row and sat myself down right next to her. Remember, she was sleeping, so I made it an extra-special point to be especially quiet, so as not to disturb her.

Then I elbowed her in the ribs.

Now, what happened next was a little surprising, because I've always heard that deaf people have a heightened sense of vision and smell, just like blind people are supposed to have a heightened sense of hearing and smell, and so on. One sense is supposed to compensate for the other, right? But that couldn't have been true, I realized, because Marlee Matlin's sense of vision wasn't so hot. She took one look at me and just assumed I was her interpreter. Of all people, you'd think she would have been able to tell the difference, but my cover wasn't blown just yet. She gave me a look that said she was terribly annoyed with me, her interpreter, for having elbowed her in the ribs.

At any rate, that's how I interpreted her response.

Then Marlee Matlin made a low, moaning kind of noise that might have been a line from *The Elephant Man* or *The Miracle Worker* or *The Hunchback of Notre Dame*.

I couldn't think what to do or say at this point, so I started making some furious hand gestures. This is what you do when you're stuck in a tense moment with a deaf person. If I couldn't make myself understood in my own language, I would make the extra-effort and communicate in hers, so I made an OK signal with my right hand, and poked my left forefinger through the hole, over and over. I hoped she would take some comfort in this, because I seemed to remember that this was the universal sign for asking a deaf person out on a date. Then I cupped my right fist, as if it was gripping a cock, and pretended to pound it against my pursed lips, also over and over. I seemed to remember that this was the universal sign for asking a deaf person if she'd like to get to know you better. Then, after a while of this, I didn't trust that I was effectively communicating my offer of friendship, so I started sticking my tongue in and out of my mouth and in the direction of my cupped fist that was meant to be gripping an imaginary cock. I wanted to emphasize the point that I really, really wanted to be her pal.

Apparently, something was lost in the translation, because poor Marlee Matlin took great offense at these gestures of friendship, and she grunted another few lines from *The Elephant Man* or *The Miracle Worker* or *The Hunchback of Notre Dame*. Then she reached for the Call button above her seat, thinking perhaps the stewardess could save her from this unpleasantness.

Now, before you go off and tell all of your Facebook friends that Gilbert Gottfried is a filthy, despicable misogynist who's so pleased with himself that he can cast aspersions in the direction of all womankind, even a handicapped woman who can't defend herself without an interpreter, please note that I was once named by the editors of a magazine as one of the Top 50 Unsexiest People in the World. Take note . . . and *then* you can go telling your friends and relations that Gilbert Gottfried is a filthy, despicable misogynist. Not only was I named to this Top 50 list, I was number one, which I guess could also mean that I was at the very bottom of the list. I was even lower than Osama bin Laden. It's one of my biggest accomplishments, and the good news here is that the list wasn't published just once in the pages of this one magazine. It was picked up by news organizations all over the place.

At first, I was a little insulted by this particular kind of attention, but then as I became more and more known for my appearance at the very top of the list—er . . . the very *bottom*—I decided to take another, more positive view. I was the best, after all. The best at being unsavory. The most unpleasant. The biggest turnoff. I ended up getting more press out of my appearance on that list than anything else I ever did. It even turned up in newspapers in Russia and India and China, just to make sure I wouldn't get laid anywhere in the world. Not that I needed any help *not* getting laid, because by this point I'd pretty much become an expert in the field.

One final point, before moving on: now that I've spent these past few pages demeaning all of these women, I can't help but wonder if there is an alternate universe, anywhere in the cosmos, where a group of tiny, whiny starlets are sitting around sipping lattes and waxing nostalgic about the leading men they never had. I can close my eyes and picture it (especially the waxing part). Cindy Crawford is sitting at a table with Elle Macpherson and Halle Berry and Michelle Pfeiffer, going on and on about . . . me! Don't laugh. It's not so far-fetched. It's merely fetched. It could happen. It could be that, right now, Cindy Crawford is sitting down with her girlfriends, saying, "Oh my gosh, do you think I have a chance to suck Gilbert Gottfried's dick? Nothing would make me happier, or feel more complete as a woman. Ever since I got my first *Vogue* cover, this has been my dream. Fingers crossed, girls!"

It's a nice picture, don't you think? Just give me a moment while it comes into focus.

I think we can all agree that there's certainly a strange little dance that comes along with being famous. And, it's certainly fun to watch as we hopeful celebrities scramble up and down that damn ladder—especially during the Academy Awards, when they start showing the annual dead person montage. As celebrity barometers go, this one's pretty telling. I look forward to it all year long. I read the obituaries or listen to the news and think, *Oh, this guy won't make it onto the dead person montage.* Or, *This guy will probably get a full-screen tribute.* For the bottom-rung celebrities, they usually put a bunch of smaller stills into the same frame, but the top-rung stars get our undivided attention. The really, really big stars sometimes get a whole clip, to open or close the segment, and it's usually followed by a loud and sustained applause.

Just this past year, for example, Kathryn Grayson died a week or so before the Oscar broadcast and I caught myself wondering if she'd make the cut. Now, chances are you're reading this and thinking, *Who the hell is Kathryn Grayson?* Well, she was an actress and opera singer who appeared in a bunch of movie musicals, including *Anchors Aweigh,* with Frank Sinatra. If you didn't grow up sleeping on the couch in your parents' living room, staying up until all hours watching movies on the black-and-white television, there's a good chance you might never have heard of Kathryn Grayson, but that wasn't me. I couldn't say with any great degree of certainty, but there's a good chance I jerked off to her, at one time or another. At some point during her career, she might have topped out at #314 on our celebrity depth chart, although to be fair there were probably only six or seven hundred celebrities at the time. However, at the time of her death Kathryn Grayson was probably charting at #3,000, give or take a couple rungs.

Farrah Fawcett? She'd spent a couple years in the double digits, at the upper reaches of fame, so you'd think she'd be remembered on Oscar night for her work in *Sunburn* and *The Cannonball Run*. As it turned out, though, the folks in charge of the dead person montage that year didn't even think poor Farrah deserving.

Go figure.

It's a fickle business, show business. For Hollywood stars like myself, our place on the celebrity ladder is only as secure as our last hit movie, our last sold-out show, our last scathingly funny performance at a Friars Club roast.

I can only hope that when my time is up and I've told my last offensive joke, the folks in charge of the dead person montage will honor me and my life's work with an appropriate tribute. Right now, I'm thinking a still from *Hot to Trot,* the Bobcat Goldthwait starrer, would be a fine and fitting send-off. It didn't exactly launch my career, that picture, but it didn't kill it—and, if you've paid any attention to my career over the years, you'll know that's saying something.

Clip 'n' Save Joke no. 11 ✂

A Jew, an Italian, a Polish guy and a midget walk into a bar. The bartender says, "What is this, a joke?"

Clip 'n' Save Joke no. 12 ✂

A nurse walks into the doctor's office and says, "The Invisible Man is here." The doctor says, "Tell him I can't see him."

Clip 'n' Save Joke no. 13 ✂

A guy says to his girlfriend, "you've got a tight twat and no tits." So the girlfriend says, "Get off my back."

11

Cheating Death

You haven't lived until you've had a near-death experience. I know this because I've had two of them, although most people would only count the first, and even then they'd argue that I didn't come close enough to dying to start writing books about it. They'd also argue that I didn't come close enough to dying because I'm still here, not dead.

There's no pleasing some people, is there?

Before I go any further with this line of thought, I offer a word of caution. Or maybe it's a word of apology. To be accurate, it's not just *one* word, it's quite a few, and here they are (in no particular order): it troubles me, a little bit, whenever a semi-celebrity like myself comes out in public and thumps his chest and boasts that he has survived some terrible ordeal or illness or accident, as I am apparently doing here. (I can't help myself!) It's a slippery slope—and if you've never been on a slippery slope, trust me, it can get pretty slippery. If you're not careful, you might hurt yourself.

You see it in the semi-celebrity press all the time. Someone who can't even get booked on *The Wendy Williams Show* (which, if you're not familiar with it, is kind of like *The Arsenio*

Hall Show with bad hair), winds up on the cover of *People* magazine, announcing he or she has survived a near-death experience, like it was some sort of career move. That's not me. (Oh, *please*, don't let that be me.) I'm not some poor schmuck talking trash about beating cancer or tonsillitis or anal warts. Whenever I see that, I start to think the disease is listening in and getting angry. It's just a matter of time. It's like when someone is in a street fight, getting his ass kicked, and then the guy who's doing the ass kicking decides he's handed out enough of a beating or maybe he's just bored so he starts to walk away. And then the person who was getting his ass kicked grows a pair and stands up and shouts, "Yeah, you better walk away, you fucking pussy!" And then whoever it is doing the beating gets pissed and comes back and finishes the job. I feel that way about any disease. It's never a good idea to piss it off.

Okay, so maybe I am that schmuck, but I'm hoping no one will notice. (Let's just keep this between us, if you don't mind.) If I was doing this on the cover of *People* magazine, it would be hard not to call attention to myself and my struggles, but here in the pages of this book I should be all right. This being a book by Gilbert Gottfried, I'm pretty sure no one is going to read it anyway.

Once again, I'll follow the lead of my nodding celebrity acquaintance Julie Andrews and start at the beginning. (And by *nodding* I mean she shakes her head from side-to-side whenever I get too close to her at an industry event.) Julie Andrews doesn't just sing, you know. She also writes books, so she knows about things like pacing and structure. Plus, there's a reason why the expression *first things first* is so much more popular than the hardly used *first things second*, so I'm going with the crowd on this one.

Oh, wait: I just remembered a Julie Andrews story, and I'm thinking that as long as she now shows up twice in these pages there should at least be a story attached to one of her appearances. This one took place soon after September 11, and airport security had become really tight, so I was going through a fairly thorough search before being allowed through the gate. Don't misunderstand, it wasn't a full, anal-cavity-type search—those only happened on Mondays, I was told—but let's just say my luggage was being violated. The interesting thing about this particular search was that the security people knew who I was. One of the guys said, "Oh, you're Gilbert Gottfried!" As if I needed to hear this from *him*. Then he proceeded to rattle off a list of my credits, coming up with movies I'd been in that I didn't remember at all. He knew my career better than me, and the whole time he was rattling off my credits he and his co-workers were going through my suitcase and patting me down.

Finally, I said, "You know who I am. You've seen all my movies. And you still have to search me?"

So the guy said, "Oh, don't be offended by that. We did the same thing to Julie Andrews yesterday."

It's not much of a story, I know, but at least it's a story.

Okay, now if you don't mind I'll get back to the *real* story I was telling before I so rudely interrupted myself—the one about me sidestepping death. First, around the time I was recording my voice-over part for *Aladdin,* I began to feel terribly sick. Along with the terrible sickness came a terrible worry. It had nothing to do with my role in *Aladdin,* this sickness, or with my uncertain career prospects. Mostly, it's that it wasn't like me to feel so terribly sick. More likely, I was the one inducing terrible sickness in others, but I was having severe stomachaches. I believe the technical term for it is *intense abdominal pain*, which sounds much more serious. Also, I was getting the chills and shaking like crazy. I believe the technical term for this is *getting the chills and shaking like crazy*, which sounds pretty much the same.

I should mention here that I had previously experienced enough success in show business that I could afford to move out of my mother's apartment and into a place of my own. It was at this point I realized I was no longer a stupid, immature little boy. I was now a stupid, immature adult. This happened some years before the onset of my terrible sickness, mind you, but much later than you might think. I had only experienced some modest success, minding you again, which meant I could only afford a modest apartment. I still slept on the couch in front of the television in the living room, but at least it was my own couch in my own living room. It wasn't a particularly nice couch, or a particularly nice living room, but it was mine.

Regrettably, I now had to make my own snacks.

The reason I should mention this is because I was alone. A nice Jewish boy like me, in the middle of such a terrible sickness, is used to having his mother tell him what to do, but my mother was in a different apartment, so for a few days I didn't know what to do. Finally, I went to see the doctor.

This was a smart decision, it turned out, although I followed it with a not-so-smart decision. As soon as I got to the doctor's office, I asked to use the bathroom. It didn't occur to me that the doctor might need a urine sample until I was standing over the toilet, finishing my business. I felt like such an idiot I could have slapped my palm against my forehead, like in one of those V-8 vegetable juice commercials, but in order to do that I would have had to let go of my dick and I might have peed all over the wall. Plus, I usually don't like to let go of my dick unless I absolutely have to, so it struck me just then as an unnecessary gesture.

So what did I do? I went back to the waiting room and hoped there'd be enough time for me to produce another few drops of urine before the doctor was ready to see me. It was one of the few times in recorded medical history when a patient was hoping there'd be a long wait—but, as it turned out, it wasn't quite long enough. I went in to see the doctor and he started examining me. He asked me a bunch of questions. Most of these questions I'd already answered on the pages and pages of paperwork I had to fill out in the waiting room, but he asked them anyway. In medical school, they call this being thorough. Then he took some blood samples—also, thorough. Then he handed me a cup and asked for a urine sample.

Like a good patient, I went to the bathroom to see if I could come up with anything. I tried and tried, with no luck. I must have been taking a long time, or making a dreadful commotion, because after a while one of the nurses started pounding on the bathroom door.

"Mr. Gottfried!" she said, excitedly. "Mr. Gottfried, are you all right in there?"

I put my dick back in my pants and opened the bathroom door a crack and explained the problem.

The nurse said, "Run the sink. Sometimes that helps."

So I closed the door and ran the sink. This time, it didn't help, so I went out to see the nurse for some more of her professional advice.

She said, "Drink some water. Sometimes that helps."

So I drank some water and waited to see if it would help. It didn't, so I went back out to the reception area to see if they had any magazines. You know, maybe some firefighter magazines, with centerfolds of rushing water or open hydrants to inspire me. The great fountains of Europe. Dolphins splashing around in the ocean. Something. A time like this, an establishment like that, you'd think there'd be some urine porn to help a fellow out . . . but there was nothing. Not even an old *Sports Illustrated* swimsuit issue, where I could have at least gotten off on all those pictures of beaches.

I never felt so all alone.

Or, dry.

Then, to make matters worse, I got the chills. All of a sudden, I was shaking, shivering . . . you might even say I was *shuddering.* Whatever you call it, there was quite a lot of unsettling movement going on, and on one of my trips out to the nurse for some urine sample advice she became concerned.

Soon, the doctor was concerned as well. He said, "Gilbert, we need to get you to the hospital."

Next thing I knew, I was racing through traffic in a cab. This was a sign that something was horribly wrong, because I never take cabs. Another person might have been troubled by being sent to the emergency room, but the money on the meter was a much bigger concern to me just then. Also, I didn't know how much I was supposed to tip the driver.

For the next three days, I lay in a hospital bed with a high fever and chills. My mother visited. My sisters visited. At first, the doctors didn't know what was wrong with me. It wasn't just that I seemed a little odd or eccentric. They decided I had a burst appendix, which seemed to me like something they should have seen right away. I mean, I'm no doctor, but you'd think a thing like a burst appendix should be easy to diagnose. But it wasn't the diagnosis that was giving these medical professionals trouble, it turned out. It was wondering how much damage had been done by the bursting.

Happily, I had some experience in this area. Usually, when one of my organs bursts, there's quite a lot of noise and fuss, only here there was no way to know the result of all that noise and fuss, or the reasons behind it. (Also, there can sometimes be a small mess, requiring a damp cloth or some tissues.)

As long as I was stable, the doctors said they wanted to determine what was going on with my insides before cutting me open. I guess this was important, and thorough, because of course they wanted to know where to cut, so we waited and waited while they determined and determined. I remember feeling incredibly anxious in the middle of all this waiting and waiting, which was a whole lot more tension-filled than my usual state of being just regular anxious. My doctors didn't exactly have the best bedside manner. They knew what they were doing, apparently, but setting me at ease wasn't too high on their list of priorities. At one point, one of my doctors said, "We've got no idea what the extent of the damage was, Gilbert. We might have to cut out some of your intestine when we open you up, and you'll have to wear a colostomy bag."

He said this like wearing a colostomy bag was a casual, everyday thing, like he was telling me I might have to wear my hair a bit shorter on one side of my head—although, now that I've made this comparison I'm realizing it wasn't like that at all. I've been to barbershops where I've been told just that with a great deal more feeling than I got from this doctor about having to wear a colostomy bag.

My first thought was about the stand-up comic I used to know when I was just starting out, the guy whose colostomy bag burst while he was banging some girl on the stage at the Comic Strip. I thought, *I don't want to be like that guy.*

(Of course, one of the reasons I didn't want to be like that guy was because his career was in the toilet, which I could only assume he still carried around with him at the side of his leg.)

My second thought was about the girl he was banging. I wondered if there was some way to get in touch with her, but then I thought, *Nah . . . she's probably old, or married, or covered with shit.*

Then I thought, *Hey, I wonder if she has a younger sister.*

Anyway, they did the surgery. As a result of all that determining, they determined that I had peritonitis, which is an inflammation of the peritoneum. All this time, I didn't even know I had one of those, and now it was inflamed. If I'd waited another day or two before going to the doctor, I could have died. At least, this is what the doctors told me, with their wonderful bedside manner—and, naturally, this was what I started telling women, under the impression that it would entitle me to sympathy sex.

So now the doctors knew where to cut, and what to cut, which was a good and welcome thing. They fixed me up. Another good and welcome thing: I didn't have to wear a colostomy bag, but it was still pretty disgusting. I lay there for days and days with my stomach hanging open, because they were worried about an infection. Once again, I'm no doctor, but you'd think with an open wound like that, you might want to close it if you're so worried about an infection, or cover it with a giant Band-Aid. But what the hell did I know?

I ended up staying in the intensive care unit for almost a month. A few of my friends came to visit after the surgery—and by *a few* I mean the one or two I'd managed to collect to that point in my life. (Okay, maybe it was three or four . . . but who's counting?) Howard Stern, the King of All Media, came to visit. He didn't want to be noticed, coming in and out of the hospital, so he put on sunglasses and a baseball cap, which even in the middle of my pain and suffering struck me as the stupidest fucking thing I'd ever seen. After all, he's a ridiculously tall person, with a ridiculously wild head of hair, so it's not like a pair of sunglasses and a baseball cap are much of a disguise. It reminded me of those old movies where someone puts on a pair of glasses to change his appearance, like Clark Kent used to do when he didn't want to be mistaken for Superman.

At eight-feet tall, with that great big nose, it looked like the number 7 was visiting me, but I recognized Howard right away. It helped, I guess, that I knew he'd be coming, because Robin Quivers had visited a day or two before, and they needed something new to talk about on the air. This way, at least, they could compare notes and fill a couple segments.

I don't think Howard particularly wanted to be there. He didn't say much, and he didn't stay long. He took one look at my open stomach and turned red. Or blue. Or white. Some color he wasn't supposed to turn. He said, "Gilbert, that's the most disgusting thing I've ever seen. You expect people to visit you, looking like that?"

Right before he left, Howard asked if there was anything he could bring me. My eyes filled up with tears, the way they do whenever I think I'll be receiving some free shit. I ran through a long list of things I thought I could use, and I kept updating that list from week-to-week, until finally Howard just sent me a two-dollar pair of slippers and called it quits, and he never again made the mistake of asking me if I needed anything.

Richard Belzer came to visit, almost every day. This was back before he was a serious actor, so he had some time on his hands. He'd come in, say hello, and sit down at the foot of my bed. Then he'd read the newspaper. He wouldn't even talk to me. After a while, he'd set the paper down and looked around the room to see if I had any magazines, only he was never all that interested in my firefighter or great fountains of Europe magazines so he'd usually just leave.

Penn Jillette came to see me, which surprised me because we didn't really know each other back then. He'd yelled at me a time or two, for trying to get Teller to talk. (I kept thinking if I squeezed him in just the right way, the guy would have to say *something* . . . eventually.) Mostly, I think Penn was curious about what had happened to me. He's got a sick, perverted mind, which is saying a lot coming from a sick, perverted guy like me. Penn was the only person who didn't recoil in shock when he looked at my stomach. He just stood over my bed like he was at a museum and I was the exhibit. He looked me over carefully, from every angle. Then he said, "You survived what killed Houdini." Like it was a badge of honor.

One of my favorite parts of the hospital routine was the way a nurse or doctor would come in every day to ask if I'd broken wind. I'd always ask, "Why, have the other patients been complaining?"

After I was there for a while, I learned that the reason they kept asking was to determine my overall health, which means that if farting is a sign of health I'll probably live forever.

One thing about spending all that time in the intensive care unit: there's no such thing as shame. Or maybe there is, but nobody cares. There were all these people coming by—doctors, nurses, perverted magicians—and I was hanging out there for all the world to see, at all hours, day and night. People were poking me, examining me, trying not to laugh or cringe or puke. But I didn't care. Everybody had seen everything by this point, in some cases far more than they cared to see. Once, a big black nurse came into my room and took one look at me lying on the bed, with my sheets thrown every which way, and said, "Cover yourself up, young man. I can see your jingle bells."

No one had ever called them that before. I secretly hoped it would catch on.

Another time, a priest came by to see how I was doing. At first I thought it was Stern, dressed for a bit, or maybe trying out a new disguise, but it was a real priest. I know this because he fondled my jingle bells—and, when I reached to fondle his, he didn't shoo my hand away, as so often happens.

The priest told me a story that made no sense, in a high-pitched Irish accent. It's like he was sent from Central Casting, but only after the more reasonable-looking priests had been sent out on other calls. Then I told him that I was Jewish, in a high-pitched Brooklyn accent, which to him must have sounded like a story that made no sense.

After I was released, I continued to visit my primary doctor on a regular basis. He'd check my wound and change my dressing and tell me how I was doing, but I didn't need him to tell me how I was doing. I could tell just by looking in the mirror. I looked like the Octomom, and this was long before we even knew about the Octomom. (We could only imagine.) My stomach was pushed all the way out into the middle of the room. When I walked, I waddled—which I suppose was good practice for my future role as the Aflac duck. The only good or encouraging thing about my appearance was that if things didn't work out for me in stand-up comedy, I could always find work in a circus sideshow.

Finally, I had to ask if I could expect any improvement. I said, "Doc, will my stomach go down? It's hanging out into the middle of the room."

He looked me over and shrugged his shoulders as if he couldn't have cared less and said, "It's gone down as much as it's going to."

Again with the bedside manner.

I said, "You mean that's it? This is what I'm gonna look like for the rest of my life?"

He said, "Pretty much."

I said, "There's nothing you can do?"

He looked me over one more time and seemed to give the matter some thought. Then he said, "Well, if you're *vain*, there's an operation we could try."

The way he said the word *vain* it sounded like one of the original sins, when really it was just me not wanting to look like the Octomom, which I guess meant it was more like a new and improved sin. It's not like I wanted to get my nose shaped, or a cleft put into my chin. I just wanted to look like a regular person. I had a hard enough time getting laid before my stomach reached all the way into the middle of the room.

So I had the operation, which was classified by my insurance company as cosmetic surgery, but then a couple years later they had to do a follow-up procedure because the area had become infected, and this, too, was classified as cosmetic surgery.

Now whenever I tell people I've had two cosmetic surgeries they step back and squint, like I'm trying to put one over on them. They look me up and down and say, "Really, what did you look like before?" Then they ask me to turn and face the other way—not because they want to see if I've had any work done on my ass, but because they seem to prefer it when I turn and face the other way.

Some months after my long stay in the intensive care unit, I ran into one of my doctors on the street outside the hospital. Me and my peritoneum were out for a stroll, and a gentleman approached me and said he was one of the doctors who had been in the operating room with me. When he introduced himself, I wondered what was expected of me in this interaction. I thought maybe the man wanted some sort of gratuity, or perhaps a character reference, but it turned out he just wanted to say hello, so now I had to make polite conversation with a man who had seen my insides.

I said, "How did I look in there?"

He said, "Let's put it this way. You're a very lucky man."

I wasn't so sure what he meant by this, but since he put it

that way, who was I to argue? Besides, I couldn't even be certain that this man was a doctor. He wasn't wearing a white coat or a hospital ID. He stuck his finger up my ass, but that didn't prove anything. It's possible he was just trying to be helpful. Nevertheless, I decided to take him at his word and consider myself lucky.

Okay, so that was my first near-death experience. It's not much of a story, I realize, but it was certainly gross and disgusting. This next near-death experience was a lot less gross and disgusting, which was just as well. It took place in Los Angeles, backstage at *The Tonight Show.* For a number of years, after Jay Leno took over from Johnny Carson, which is not to be confused with the period of time after Jay Leno took over from Conan O'Brien, I was a semi-regular on the show, but only for bits and sketches and not-so-special occasions. It was like being one of the "Mighty Carson Art Players," only there was no Carson and we weren't so mighty. Every so often, I'd get a call from one of the producers, asking me if I could fly out for an appearance. Sometimes, they'd want me to fly out that day. Sometimes, it would be the next day. Very often, I'd be out in Los Angeles already, taping *Hollywood Squares* or pursuing some other piece of show business, so I'd just wander over to the studio.

There would always be a script waiting for me in my dressing room, but I made it a special point not to learn my lines. I believed it got in the way of my performance. Typically, the sketches were a whole lot funnier when I had no idea what I was doing. I played Queen Elizabeth. I played Yoda and Harry Potter. I even played Kim Jong-il. In fact, it was when I played the North Korean dictator that I got into some trouble with certain Asian antidefamation groups, and the funny thing was they didn't even put me in makeup to look like him. There was enough of a resemblance already, so I just wore a general's outfit and a big pair of glasses, but that didn't stop all these watchdog groups from complaining to NBC executives for hiring an American actor and exaggerating his squinty eyes and big teeth. Who could have predicted when I was a nice Jewish boy living up in Brooklyn that I would one day grow up to be an offensive Asian stereotype?

The near-death part of my *Tonight Show* experience happened in my dressing room. Specifically, it happened in the bathroom just off my dressing room—which looking back should not have come as such a great surprise. You see, the *Tonight Show* dressing rooms were old. Nothing seemed to work the way it was supposed to work—the way it might have worked in, say, 1964. This particular dressing room happened to have a sliding door to the bathroom, and I'd somehow gotten stuck inside. The door wouldn't slide open.

I pounded it. I pulled it. And then after a while I realized that usually, whenever I'm in the bathroom doing any kind of pounding or pulling, there's something else going on, but this was shaping up to be a true emergency.

Another unusual thing: whenever I was in one of those dressing rooms, there was always someone coming by with something important to discuss. A production assistant. A hair and makeup person. Someone with a question or a comment or a note on my scintillating performance. But for some reason, on this day, no one came by. I pounded and pounded, but got back nothing. I pulled and pulled. Nothing. I even started screaming, but only a little. I didn't want anyone to think I was gay.

Finally, I managed to slide the door open a few inches, enough to squeeze my arm through the narrow opening. There was a phone on the other side of the door that I thought I might be able to reach, so I reached. It was on a table, up against the wall next to the sliding door. A couple inches more, and I would have been able to grab it, or at least pull on the cord and drag the phone toward me. It was like a bad scene from a bad movie, the kind I might have appeared in at the height of my career, the way it was just beyond my grasp. I kept trying and trying. I repositioned myself, every which way. I even tried the other arm, thinking one arm might be longer than the other.

If I had a pen or a pencil, I might have been able to use those extra few inches to poke at the cord or a wire and pull it closer, but of course I didn't have a pen or a pencil. I looked around the bathroom, to see if there was anything else I might use, to help with my reaching, but there was nothing, so I continued with my pounding and pulling and yelling.

This went on for five or ten minutes. I started to panic. Really, my situation went from funny to frustrating to frightening in no time at all. I began to sweat profusely. I couldn't figure out why nobody had come to my dressing room to check on me, because somebody was always coming into my dressing room to check on me. I started to have all kinds of paranoid thoughts, like maybe these *Tonight Show* people were trying to tell me something, or that they'd lured me to the NBC Studios in Burbank, California, for the sole purpose of trapping me in a backstage bathroom and having me scare myself to death.

A lesser man might have shit himself—even though there was a perfectly good toilet in the room.

For a few brief, terrifying moments, this diabolical NBC plan seemed to be working, but before I slipped into a complete, blind panic I noticed a small metal trash can in the corner of the bathroom. It was too big to fit through the narrow opening I'd made in the door, but I reached for it anyway, mostly because I had run out of ideas. I picked up the trash can and started banging it against the floor, against the door, against the wall. My first thought was to make as much noise with this thing as possible. And, really, I was making quite a racket. Surely, I thought, someone will hear me. But nobody seemed to hear me, so my second thought was to use the trash can like a hammer and try to bust my way out. Surely, I thought, some NBC accountant-type would come by and admonish me for destroying company property. But there were no NBC accountant-types.

At this point, I was pounding and banging with such reckless abandon that the paint started to chip away off the walls. Then, some bits of plaster. Once again, if this had been a bad scene in a bad movie, this would have been the part where a thin sliver of sunlight would peek through the small opening I was making with this trash can. Or maybe there'd be some hopeful music playing in the background.

But there was no hopeful music or ray of sunshine. Just a tiny, frenzied Jew, banging away at the cheap walls of a backstage dressing room, over and over.

Finally—thankfully!—I managed to bust through the walls in such a way that I could crawl through the small opening I'd made. There was plaster dust everywhere, and little bits of wood and plasterboard and whatever else they put in dressing room walls back in 1964. I pushed my way through like I was the Incredible Hulk, and I half-expected to be met at the other side by cheering and confetti. Certainly, it was cause for celebration, but there was no celebration. I thought it would be like one of those dramatic survival stories they show on the television news, where someone emerges from a mine or a cave or a mountain of rubble and the entire town has gathered to welcome them to safety, but nobody noticed, or cared.

A short while later, after I'd told a few people what had happened, some *Tonight Show* staffers came by to look at the hole I'd made in my dressing room wall. Someone even brought Jay Leno by to look at it, and he just shook his head and walked away.

Next, a reporter from the *National Enquirer* came by to interview me, and ended up running a story comparing me to the Incredible Hulk, which I thought was flattering. The reporter came because I called the *National Enquirer* office to give them a scoop. It was the first piece of positive press I'd gotten in the *Enquirer* in my entire career, and for a moment I thought it might lead to some exciting new opportunities for me in the movies. Some producer would read about me breaking out of my dressing room like the Incredible Hulk and think to cast me as the lead in an action-adventure picture. It was only a matter of time. After all, I'd already cheated death—not just once, but twice. I'd survived a horrible disfigurement. I'd busted through a wall in a fit of blind rage and fury.

Now all that was left was for me to get the girl.

A successful businessman in his later years thinks about his glory days as a soldier in World War II. In particular, he remembers a quaint little coffee shop in Bavaria, where he had the most delicious Bavarian cream pie. All he can think about is how much he would like to taste this Bavarian cream pie again. Nothing he's tasted in all these years can come close to it.

So he gathers his money, and buys a plane ticket to Bavaria. The plane loses one of its wings and crashes into the ocean. As the plane sinks deeper and deeper into the sea, the man pries open the cockpit door and manages to escape. He finds a piece of driftwood and holds on for dear life through some of the worst thunderstorms and tidal waves the ocean has seen. He even gets attacked by a school of sharks, and manages to fight them off.

Eventually, he makes it to land, where he now must travel through the forest, being attacked by animals. Once again, he somehow manages to survive, although he's lost a lot of blood, and has suffered grave injuries and is now extremely weak. At some point, he decides to give up. It's no use, he thinks, and he looks for a place where he might lie down and die.

Just then, he notices a light off in the distance, and he realizes it's the Bavarian coffee shop he remembers from World War II. He gathers up all his strength, and somehow manages to crawl on his hands and knees to the coffee shop. With his last ounce of will and energy, he lifts himself up onto a chair by a table.

A waiter comes over and hands him a menu.

The man says, through a raspy, weak voice, "Dear God, please. All I want is one tiny slice of your Bavarian cream pie."

The waiter says, "I'm sorry, but we're all out of Bavarian cream pie."

So the man says, "Well, okay. How's the apple?"

12

Just Tugging Along

I made a big splash at the 1991 Emmy Awards. This might come as a surprise to careful readers, who will be quick to point out that I have never done anything in my career to deserve an award of any kind, even one that's voted on by my degenerate peers. It's also surprising because as far as most people know they don't have a swimming pool at the Emmys.

But here's an interesting loophole: you don't have to win anything to go to the Emmys. You don't have to be nominated. You can simply appear on the awards broadcast as a *presenter*, which means your agent is able to get you a fifteen-second walk-on role, in exchange for naming rights to his or her firstborn son. Also, a lifetime supply of microwave popcorn. Apparently, there's a lot of backstage horse-trading going on at these awards shows that has nothing to do with actually winning an award or earning the respect of your peers. It doesn't even have anything to do with horses.

So there I was, undeserving as usual, showing up at the theater in a handsome tuxedo, ready to make what would turn out to be one of the more memorable appearances of my forgettable career, although to judge from how the night started out it might have passed unnoticed. You see, there was no side entrance into the theater, which meant the only way in was to walk down the red carpet, which in turn offered a small humiliation for someone like me. It wasn't a big humiliation, mind you, but if you're like me you'll agree that indignity is a dish best served with a side of ice cream.

(I don't actually know what that last line means, but it sounds like something Bogie might have said in one of his lesser films.)

On either side of the red carpet there were dozens and dozens of reporters and photographers. The press was everywhere, only they weren't so interested in me. This alone wasn't so unusual, except their disinterest had never been so plain. I was like Kryptonite, to these hardworking people and the tools of their trade. When I arrived on the carpet, there were all these cameras going off, and microphones being shoved into the aisle, and flashbulbs popping, but as soon as I stepped on that damn rug everything just stopped. It's like the bottoms of my shoes had some anticelebrity remote control sensors, and as soon as they touched the carpet all the mechanisms of fame magically shut down.

I pretended not to notice, and I strode purposefully down that carpet as if my career depended on it. Meanwhile, the press pretended not to notice, too—as if *their* careers depended on it. In fact, some of them even held up signs saying, "Pay no attention to that impish Jew, strolling the carpet in his handsome tuxedo! He's not worthy of our attention! He's merely a *presenter!*"

At first, I thought all of this raging disinterest had to do with my lowly *presenter* status, but then I realized it was just me. There were other presenters walking that red carpet, stopping to pose for pictures or talk to reporters, but if it looked to a member of the press like I might stop or even slow down he or she would make a motion to suggest that I keep moving.

One of the other presenters that night was Sam Kinison, but for some reason everyone was paying attention to *him*. Nothing against Sam, who was of course a brilliant comedian. This was before he died. After he died, he was too busy to be a mere presenter at the Emmy Awards. Also, he was no longer such a brilliant comedian. His timing was off, if you want to know the truth. On this night, though, his pending appearance was the talk of the production meetings. He was just a presenter, like me, but he was still the center of attention, even though his tuxedo was not nearly as handsome as mine. Everyone was worried he would say or do something to disrupt the show, but it wasn't Sam they had to worry about. It was me, the impish Jew.

The awards show people, the network, the producers . . . everyone was so worried about crazy Sam Kinison, but I was stealth. That is how I roll, apparently. (Mind you, this was news to me, but I was happily surprised.) Under the radar, that's where you'll find me, I've learned, and if you can't find me there be sure to check under the kitchen table, or perhaps the bed. These nervous entertainment executives didn't see me coming, which is usually how I like it when I come (note, please, the family-friendly spelling), and there had been a few things on my mind that I wanted to get off my chest.

What was troubling me was this: Pee-wee Herman. Specifically, I was troubled about Pee-wee's troubles with the law. Remember, this was around the time he'd been arrested at a porn theater in Florida, for the simple crime of doing what people are supposed to be doing at porn theaters in Florida. It's part of our unwritten social contract, that we confine our semipublic acts of masturbation and self-flagellation to the semidarkness of our local porn theater, where that type of behavior belongs. (If it works out that you're able to confine your alleged misconduct to a strip mall in Florida, so much the better.)

Our pal Pee-wee was only doing his part, showing a childlike curiosity in sexual matters, and what happened? Well, no sooner than you can say, "Gee, that guy on the screen must shave his balls," Pee-wee was getting arrested for playing with his pee-wee.

(Sorry, I couldn't resist.)

(But then, neither could Pee-wee.)

Predictably, this was front-page news. Every news and entertainment program led with a mug shot of Paul Reubens, looking solemn and unrecognizable and abashed, which is not a description you often see in this context but now that I'm a writer I figured it's okay to branch out.

(Gotta love that guy who invented the thesaurus . . . he's got a different word for *everything*.)

The arrest photo ran in every major newspaper in the country. It even made *People* magazine. It wasn't the most flattering picture—a potential career ender, if you asked me, and I happen to be something of an authority on career-ending moves. With his long hair and beard, Pee Wee looked a little like Christ, if Christ had been arrested in Florida for jerking off in a local porn theater, although now that I think of it I can't imagine Mr. Christ ever found himself in such a circumstance. I'll have to ask Mel Gibson. I understand he knows about such things.

To make matters worse, Pee-wee tried to talk his way out of it. He said to the arresting officer, "But I'm Pee-wee Herman," thinking maybe this might get him off.

(I know, I know . . . I've backed right into an obvious joke, something along the lines of *Yeah, as opposed to the other thought he'd just had that was supposed to get him off*, but it's not like me to stoop or pander, at least not without proper lubrication.)

That was just about the worst thing he could have said. The *absolute* worst thing he could have said would have been, "But I'm Gilbert Gottfried."

Which would of course have begged the natural follow-up question, from the entire vice squad, delivered in unison: "Who?"

Back to the Emmys. Before the show, I did a mike check, but Mike wasn't there.

(Again, sorry. Sometimes I just can't help myself.)

The sound check went fine. A few earnest-seeming young people told me where I was meant to stand, when I was scheduled to appear in the program, who would be introducing me. Beyond that, nothing was prepared for me. Sometimes, you go to these shows, one of the writers has prepared a bit or a line that may or may not have anything to do with the category of award you're supposed to present. And it may or may not have anything to do with contemporary American humor. It's just a bit or a line, something to say. Here, though, I appeared to be on my own. There was a list of the nominees' names, and an envelope I was meant to open, and that was it. Another young someone wearing a headset who appeared to be in a position of authority said, "Just have fun, Gilbert."

So I took him at his word.

I'm told that people are still talking about what I said that night, in my first and only appearance as an Emmy presenter. I hardly believe this is true, but it's nice to hear, and I certainly don't mind reporting it here as unsubstantiated fact.

What I said, to the best of my recollection, went a little something like this:

"I can sleep a lot better, knowing Pee-wee Herman has been arrested.

"If masturbation is a crime, then I should be on Death Row. To think that by the age of twelve, I was already Al Capone.

"Right now, my right hand is as strong as Superman's right hand. I can hold a piece of coal and squeeze it into a diamond.

"If the cops tried to arrest me, they'd be yelling, 'Stay away from his right hand! He can kill you with it!'

"How do the police even prove you were masturbating? Do they dust you for prints?"

Oh, I had a million of 'em, as we human animal comedians like to say. And I was determined to tell every last one of 'em, to the great discomfort of the show's producers and a wide swath of Middle America. What the hell did I care? And the audience at the Pasadena Civic Auditorium didn't seem to care either. In fact, they seemed to rather enjoy it. (Not just *merely* enjoy it, but *rather* enjoy it, which is a whole lot better.) They were rolling in the aisles, laughing their heads off. Frequently, this is just a meaningless expression, meant to indicate that people appreciated a performance, but in this case it's an accurate description. Betty White was one of the nominees that year, for her outstanding work on that dried-up-prune show she did with Bea Arthur, and she was rolling in the aisle in such an uncontrollable fit that someone thought to call a medic. And one of the actors from *Twin Peaks* really did laugh his head off, although in retrospect I suppose it could have been a special effect.

But seriously, folks . . . I killed. I was a regular Charles Bronson up there on that stage, gunning down this unsuspecting Emmy audience. There were peals of laughter. There were howls of merriment. There was even some pant wetting, I was later told, all of it followed by a giant wave of applause. I mention this not to tell readers how great I am or to feed my ego. (Okay, maybe a little.) No, I mention this to make a point about the press, which for the time being appeared to receive me with its usual indifference. I left the stage to hoots and hollers and guffaws, and then I was met backstage by reporters and photographers who all seemed to take turns wondering why they now had to talk to me. After all, they'd spent all that time ignoring me on my way in to the theater, so why should they now have to acknowledge me on my way out?

Normally, at that time in my career, when one of the paparazzi screamed my name, it was to tell me to move a little bit to my left because I was blocking their shot of Ted Danson. And that was still very much the case. I'd left the audience spent and exhausted from all that belly laughing, but the media couldn't have cared less. I was still ignored by the reporters and photographers. Even the autograph seekers were looking straight past me, hoping to catch a glimpse of the cast of *thirtysomething*.

At least that's how it was at first, but after a while some members of the press started to pay attention. It's possible that there was just a lull in the proceedings, and I was the only remotely famous or attention-worthy person in their line of sight, but for a moment or two I was the center of attention. Okay, maybe I wasn't the *center* of attention, not even for a moment or two, but at least I was nearby. One or two photographers actually wanted me to turn and face their cameras. One or two reporters actually shouted out questions for me to answer. I wouldn't go so far as to suggest I'd set off a media frenzy, but there was a stillness backstage at the Emmys that had more than a little something to do with me.

I was a hit, at least in Gilbert Gottfried terms—a big fat pile of steaming hit.

And then, just like that, I wasn't. Somewhere between the press room and the Governors Ball, something happened. I was feeling pretty good about myself when I left the theater and headed over to the Governors Ball, but then when I got there the governor stood and zipped his pants and asked me to leave. A few people came up to me and told me they liked my set. Even Sam Kinison came over, to tell me he loved the fact that people had been so worried about him and here I'd done this little end-around and taken some of the heat off of his performance.

(He said this in a good way, I think.)

Then he asked where I shopped for my tuxedo.

After a while, though, the tone of all this admiring small

talk seemed to shift. It was subtle at first, this shift, but it became more and more noticeable as I made my way around the room. Soon, the positive vibe felt a little bit negative, and I started to hear a buzz or a groan or a whisper of speculation that my bit might be cut from the show's West Coast feed. The show had been broadcast live in most of the country, but it had yet to air in California and some of those other states on that side of the map, and this troubled me. The reason this troubled me was unquestionably selfish. I'd killed, and I wanted the whole world to know that I killed. Even people in California, which of course was where we were at the time—and where the sight of me killing could only help my career. I didn't care all that much about censorship or double standards or any of the other big-picture issues that seemed to surface on the back of this decision to cut me from the broadcast, even though I would take up these points later on in interviews and profess moral outrage to make it appear as if I gave a shit about something bigger or other than me.

It's amazing, really, the about-face the media took in response to my appearance. At first, all these reporters and photographers had been quietly tolerant; then, they were mildly interested; now they were indignant, and offended. Suddenly, I was the guy in the Pee-wee Herman spot, in the pages of all these newspapers, and on all these news and entertainment shows. Instead of a mug shot, there was a picture of me in my handsome tuxedo, making a gesture with my right hand that I suppose could have been interpreted as masturbatory. If I had been a politician, my gestures could have been seen as emphasis-adders, to help me make an important point about taxes or health care, but since I was a comedian with a long history of dick jokes they could only be seen as the sign for jerking off.

One headline called the show "The X-Rated Emmys," and a columnist referred to my appearance as "a new low." (Personally, I kind of liked that one.) The same reporters who had ignored me on the red carpet the night before were now calling me for interviews. In some of the articles I even read that the entire Emmy audience sat in shocked, stony silence the whole time I was onstage. The only time the silence was broken, the articles said, was when the *harrumphing* crowd took turns murmuring to each other how deeply offended they were by my appearance. This was certainly not the case, but I didn't have it in me to object.

All I cared about, really, was that they weren't referring to my physical appearance, because I thought I looked smart and spiffy. And I'd just started wearing my hair a new way that was meant to be fetching.

And then a curious thing happened. The more critics and pundits and media types weighed in to tell how offended they were by my performance, the more people had a chance to be offended by my performance. Millions and millions of people who would have never seen my performance in the first place. It was another one of those delicious ironies, only this one came wrapped inside an enigma with a side of coleslaw. The bit that had been cut from the broadcast was played over and over on all these news outlets. Newspapers printed my filthy comments, almost word-for-word. The entire mainstream media seemed to be in general agreement that I was the most offensive degenerate in Hollywood, and that no caring, thinking, decent person should be subjected to my views, and then they went out of their way to make sure that every caring, thinking, decent person had a second chance to do just that.

Oh, the hypocrisy! (Such great fun, don't you think?)

I could rant and rave about this, but I don't think I will. What else is there to say? Also, I can't shake this picture in my head of Betty White rolling around on the floor and I feel a sudden urge to rub one out and it's difficult to type with just my left hand.

Clip 'n' Save Joke no. 15 ✂------------------

A woman walks into a bar and breaks into tears. She says, "My husband has just left me. He ran off with his secretary. I've never had a drink in my life, but I desperately need one now."

The bartender says, "Well, for your first drink, how about a martini? That's pretty mild." So he serves her a martini, and the woman drinks half of it and promptly passes out drunk.

A group of men see the woman lying at the bar unconscious, so they pick her up, throw her on the pool table, rip her clothes off and proceed to take turns in an all-out gang bang. This lasts for several hours.

A few days later, the woman comes back to the bar and says, "I'd like a drink."

The bartender says, "Would you like a martini?"

The woman says, "No, I tried one once. It made my cunt hurt."

13

The Air up Here

When you're starting out as a comic, you work a lot of shit jobs. I've certainly worked my share. I think I've even worked some of Bob Saget's shit jobs, but this was understandable because once he became a big television star someone had to do it. I mean, big television stars like Bob Saget just don't *do* Sweet 16s—the parties, I mean.

Birthdays, weddings, Bar Mitzvahs, corporate events . . . those are the worst, but they come with the territory. In the beginning, they're low-end birthday parties and corporate events, or you wind up working in abandoned, decrepit lofts with a bunch of folding chairs for the audience, but as you move up that celebrity ladder the stakes start to change. The venues are a little nicer. There's more money. They send a car for you—or, sometimes, a first-class plane ticket.

The whole time, as you get going on your career, you like to think you'll reach a point when you'll develop a big enough name or such a big following that you won't have to take any more of these private gigs, but you never quite get there. Or maybe you do but there's so much money being waved in front of you that you can't help but grab at it. Or maybe it's just me who never quite gets there. Anyway, with me, I'll grab at pretty much anything. Put a dollar on a stick and wave it around in front of me and I'll do whatever you ask. Except *that*. That I won't do. Certainly not for a dollar. These days, *that* will cost you two dollars, at least. *This* and *that* and *that other thing?* That runs a little steeper.

A couple years ago, long after I'd hit it "big" as a movie star, not-having-sex symbol, celebrity game show contestant and fashion trendsetter, I did a gig at the "21" club in New York. It was a birthday party for one of the heirs of William Randolph Hearst. It sounded oddly glamorous, but it turned out just to be odd. I didn't know what to make of the booking when my agent called to tell me about it, but I took the job because I heard the hamburgers were good at "21."

Again, maybe it's just me, but when I hear the term *heir* I start thinking the kid is five years old, only here the instructions were straightforward. The guest of honor was a big fan. He'd seen me doing all those Friars Club roasts, and he'd seen *The Aristocrats,* and he was said to have a really wild sense of humor. The guy really *got* me, I was told.

"Go crazy, Gilbert," the heir's assistant informed me when he briefed me on the party. "This guy can take it."

So I took the assistant at his word. You don't have to tell me more than once to go crazy. I never heard from the guest of honor on this, but the information seemed solid and I was good to go. If this guy could take it, then I could certainly dish it out.

When I got to the club it looked like a throwback scene from some Marx Brothers or Three Stooges film. All of the guests were old, old, old. And rich, rich, rich. The men were

all white-haired, and tuxedoed, and the women were wearing long gowns, and everyone was sipping martinis. I think
I even saw a few monocles. It felt for a moment like I'd been
asked to perform onboard the *Titanic*, but then I checked and
realized we were on dry land. Right away, I decided that all
the clown-fucking jokes I'd written for the roomful of five-
year-olds I was expecting would not be suitable. This worried me, at first, because I hadn't prepared anything else, so I
decided to go with the clown-fucking jokes anyway. What
the hell did I care if they were suitable?

Before I went onstage, a woman took the microphone to
make a few remarks. I had no idea who she was, but the guests
seemed to recognize her. She spoke only for a moment, but
she made a passing reference to Rosebud, which of course
was the name of the sled in *Citizen Kane,* which of course was
said to have been based on the life of William Randolph
Hearst, the deceased newspaper mogul and relative of the
guest of honor. If I was smart or clever, I might have made a
couple of Rosebud jokes myself, but far be it from me to appear smart or clever. In any case, I'd been led to assume that
such a reference would be no big deal, according to the *no
holds barred* directions I'd been given by the assistant, so I was
surprised by what happened next: people started booing. In
fact, as soon as this woman made her remark, she was booed
mercilessly—although to be honest I can't recall a situation
where someone was booed mercifully.

The woman seemed surprised, as well. She couldn't get off
the stage quickly enough, and I stepped up to take her place.
It felt to me like I was taking a bullet for her—only it was a
bullet being fired from a really, really old gun, so it wasn't

likely to penetrate the skin. I didn't know enough to put two and two together after that surprising reaction, though. Or maybe I did, and came up with *five*. Anyway, I continued on in *no holds barred* mode. I'd learned, for example, that the guest of honor was really, really old, and really, really rich, and that he'd recently married a really, really young woman, so that was a place to start. I went into a whole bit about this guy's wife hoping to get rich off her geezer husband. I said, "Once she realized her name was in the will, she encouraged her husband to take an apartment on the fiftieth floor of their building. And she was always saying, 'Hey, honey. To hell with the elevator. Let's walk up.'"

I said, "Sometimes, when he's sleeping, she'll come into the room and fire a gun in the air."

I rattled off a whole bunch of gold digger jokes, each one louder and lewder and more inappropriate than the one before, and I don't think I noticed that no one was laughing. Or maybe I did notice, but I don't think I cared. The more inappropriate, I thought, the better. It was the "21" club, after all. They were paying me well. So I kept at it, and as I did the mood of the room became more and more uncomfortable. I looked out across the crowd and saw everyone's jaw hanging open—and it wasn't just to make room for those fat, juicy hamburgers.

Finally, I ran out of jokes. My time was up. So I stepped from the stage and crossed to the back of the room. No one would look at me. Everyone just sat there, all white-haired and monocled and stony-faced. Except one guy who came up to me afterward and asked if I'd like to meet the guest of honor. Just then, I didn't think this was such a good idea, but

I remembered that the assistant had said his boss had a sense of humor, and that I should feel free to say whatever I wanted. He'd said this guy could take it.

So I said, "Sure, what the hell. Bring me over."

My plan was to just wish the guy a happy birthday and get the hell out of there. He was paying me a lot of money, and I didn't want to appear rude, but when I walked over to him I noticed he wasn't all there. Actually, he wasn't there at all. Physically, he was in the room, but that was about where it ended for him. He was completely out of it. I seem to remember that he was in a wheelchair, but I can't be certain. He'd apparently just had a series of severe strokes. He was sitting with a woman who appeared to be his full-time aide, whose job was to wipe the drool off his face as he stared into thin air.

A lesser man might have been embarrassed or humiliated by this discovery, but as I have by now indicated there are no lesser men than me. Plus, the heir to the Hearst fortune didn't appear embarrassed or humiliated, so why should I? Instead, I was outraged because this seemed to me the sort of thing the assistant might have told me when he briefed me about my performance. I mean, this was information I could have certainly used in my act. I was dying out there. I had a whole bunch of gold digger–stroke victim–drool cup jokes I could have used.

Another time, I thought I was dying when in reality I was killing. There's a difference, you know. This was at a birthday party in Los Angeles—on Yom Kippur, no less. The holiest day on the Jewish calendar. This presented a problem, at first, until I told my agent that since the gig fell on the one day of the year we Jews were not supposed to work, I'd have to charge a little bit more.

The client was Kareem Abdul-Jabbar, who made the call to my agent himself. He was throwing his own party. He told my agent he was my biggest fan. (It's possible he meant he was my tallest fan, but he was certainly enthusiastic.) It would have been easy to say the same thing right back to him, the first time we met, but as I've written I didn't know the first thing about sports. I didn't even know the second or third things. The fourth thing, I happened to know, and it turned out that the fourth thing was that Kareem Abdul-Jabbar was an exceptionally tall black man who played basketball.

That much, I knew.

I thought, *A birthday party for Kareem Abdul-Jabbar, on Yom Kippur . . . this I have to do.* If nothing else, I could get a chapter out of it for my book, and it seems we have all now stumbled across the very chapter where this particular story appears.

Usually, there are ground rules. Even when there are no ground rules, like the party for William Randolph Hearst's heir, there are things I should know going in. Here, Kareem's assistant called and told me I wasn't allowed to tell any jokes about being tall, which I could only assume meant no jokes about playing basketball, either. Or, having a name no one could pronounce. It was kind of like being hired for Dolly Parton's party and told to avoid tit jokes.

Yes, Gilbert, Linda Lovelace would like you to perform at her bridal shower. Just one thing, though. No blow job jokes.

I accepted the booking and promptly forgot about it, but then a few days later I answered the phone and a voice on the other end of the line said, "Hello, Gilbert. This is Kareem Abdul-Jabbar."

I hung up, thinking it was a crank call. But after a moment it hit me what a coincidence it would be, getting a crank call from Kareem Abdul-Jabbar a couple days after Kareem Abdul-Jabbar himself had hired me to perform at his birthday party. And even if I wasn't doing the party, what crank caller in the history of the telephone would ever call someone up and claim to be Kareem Abdul-Jabbar? It had to be way down there on the list of "Do you have Prince Albert in a can?"–type gags.

Kareem called back a moment or two later and introduced himself again. This time, I didn't hang up. This time I said, "Sorry, I thought you'd sound taller."

Jump ahead to the weekend of the party. I was flown out to Los Angeles and put up at a very nice hotel. When I got there, a woman was in the lobby, organizing rides back and forth to the restaurant where the party was being held, but there was a message informing me that Kareem himself would be picking me up. Then I got another message, telling me that when Kareem arrived he'd wait for me on the left-hand side of the lobby, just a few feet from the newsstand, which seemed to me an important piece of information, because of course there was no way I would have spotted a twenty-foot black man in the lobby of my hotel if he didn't tell me exactly where he'd be standing.

The party came and I did my thing and it felt to me like I'd bombed badly. Nobody laughed. Or if they did, they did so in a quiet, subtle manner, as if they didn't want anyone else to know. I performed for only ten or fifteen minutes, but it felt to me like three or four hours. I could only imagine how long it must have felt like to Kareem Abdul-Jabbar and his friends. The minute I got offstage, I grabbed my jacket and found the woman who was organizing the rides and asked her to arrange for a car to take me back to the hotel as soon as possible. Before she could make the call, a large shadow crept over me and I looked up and saw that Kareem Abdul-Jabbar was now standing over me. I just about ruined my pants. I don't mean to suggest that I almost crapped myself. I mean that I almost came in my pants, seeing such a famous Muslim looming over me in such an up-close and intimidating way.

Kareem gently said, "Where are you going, Gilbert?"

I said, "Well, I finished my set, and I was just getting ready to go back to the hotel."

What I meant to say was, "Well, I finished my set, and I was hurrying out of here before you could find me and beat the crap out of me for ruining your party."

Kareem said, "Don't be ridiculous. A lot of people want to meet you. Come back and join the party."

So I did. Call me crazy, but when a twenty-foot black man tells you to do something you should probably think about doing it, as I learned growing up. Kareem took me around the room and introduced me to his famous friends. Most of them found something nice to say to me about my performance, although a few tried to avoid eye contact with Kareem so they wouldn't have to meet me. This was just as well, I remember thinking, because most of Kareem's friends were big and black and I seemed to recall telling a few too many jokes about big black people in my act.

Quincy Jones was there, and he came over to shake my hand. I congratulated him for fucking that blond girl from *The Mod Squad.* He seemed to appreciate my enthusiasm.

Smokey Robinson was there, although I didn't see any Miracles. I guess they couldn't get a ride to the restaurant, which you would think might be something you could easily arrange if you were a Miracle. Smokey actually came over to say hello. He hugged me. Pretty tight, as I recall. I guess maybe he was trying to squeeze tears from a clown. So I started weeping openly.

A short while later, I found myself sitting at a table, in between Kareem Abdul-Jabbar and Pamela Anderson, which I suppose would make an interesting three-way. These two majestic physical specimens would go at it, while I would sit quietly in the corner and try to come up with a specimen of my own.

At first, I was sitting at the table sneaking peeks at Pamela Anderson's breasts, but then it hit me: with Pamela Anderson, you don't have to *sneak* peeks so much as soak them in fully. Even she knows that's why she's there. Plus, even if you're only peeking, they're kind of hard to avoid. I mean, they're so *right there.*

The line of the night, though, went to Kareem Abdul-Jabbar, who turned out to be surprisingly funny for a twenty-foot-tall black man who used to sweat for a living. He leaned over to me at one point and said, "I bet you everybody in this place is wondering, *Who are those two guys with the shiksa?*"

Clip 'n' Save Joke no. 16 ✂

A Jew, an Italian and a Polish guy are working on a construction site. It's their lunch hour, so they're all sitting on a girder way up in the sky. They prepare to open their lunch boxes.

As the Italian man opens his lunch box he says, "I wonder what my wife put in here. If it's another sausage sandwich, I'm jumping off this girder and killing myself." He opens the lunch box, and finds it's a turkey sandwich, so he smiles and says, "This looks great. I love turkey."

Then the Jew says, "I wonder what my wife put in my lunch box today. If this is another meat loaf sandwich, I'm jumping off this girder to my death." He opens the lunch box and finds it's a salami sandwich, so the Jew smiles and says, "Gee, I love salami."

Finally, the Polish guy says, "I wonder what's in my lunch box. If this is another ham sandwich, I'm jumping off this girder and killing myself." He opens up the lunch box and sure enough it's a ham sandwich, so the Polish man stands up, leaps off the girder and falls to his death on the pavement below.

The Italian then turns to the Jew and says, "Why didn't he just ask his wife to make him something else?"

To which the Jew says, "He wasn't married."

GRAND FINALE

Too Soon

wo weeks after September 11, I made one of the most
talked about appearances of my career. Unfortunately, it
was two weeks after September 11, 1985, so I don't really
know why this date has any significance.

(LOL, as the kids say, which of course stands for Laugh
Out Loud. Also, JK, which stands for Just Kidding. And,
GTFOOHYCJBINFPF—Get the Fuck Out of Here You
Cheap Jew Bastard I've Never Found Particularly Funny.)

It was at a Friars Club roast for Hugh Hefner, and just to
be serious for a moment, the appearance really did take place
about two weeks after the September 11, 2001, terrorist attacks on the United States. For a while, there was some talk
about canceling the event, out of respect, but then it was
decided to go ahead with it as planned—also out of respect,
only here it was a respect for making money. For a while,
it appeared that many of the celebrities who had promised to
appear would cancel at the last minute. This was understandable. Some of them were afraid to fly, or leave their homes, or
be seen at a Friars Club roast for Hugh Hefner, who many
people believed had now been targeted by terrorists who

were a little pissed off that he continued to get more pussy than them, even at his advanced age.

But those fears about poor attendance were unfounded, it turned out. On the night of the roast, the place was packed—probably because it came around at a time when people really needed some kind of escape from the horror and terror of those days and weeks, but also because it would take a lot more than out-and-out warfare to keep a bunch of old Jews from showing up for a free meal.

One thing about these roasts: they've become a real institution. I remember watching them as a kid, edited for television. All the celebrities seemed to be having a real piss-your-pants good time, only I learned later that they used to shoot these out of sequence. Very often, they'd sit a guy like Milton Berle in a chair on the dais, and some schmuck director would say, "Okay, Mr. Berle, now we'd like you to laugh uproariously, as if you've just heard a really filthy joke." Uncle Miltie would do as he was told and laugh it up for the cameras—careful to run his famously long dick down his pant leg, so it wouldn't get in the way of the shot.

My favorite line from a Friars Club roast came to me in a once-removed sort of way. Ed McMahon told it to me. He heard it from Jack Benny, who delivered the line himself at a roast for Georgie Jessel. As far as I know, there's no footage of this particular roast, but it lives on—in *my* memory, at least, because everybody else who had anything to do with it or who saw it firsthand is probably dead: "Georgie Jessel is flying to Israel tonight," Jack Benny told the crowd, and of course he was careful to put his trademark pauses in all the right places. "You see, he has a cunt in Haifa." (Pause, pause,

pause.) Then he continued: "No, I don't mean a woman. I mean an actual cunt. He wears it for a toupee."

(Pause, pause, pause again—because with Jack Benny timing was everything.)

For a while, these roasts were presided over by my friend Jeffrey Ross, who over the years managed to convince all kinds of interesting, unlikely giants of the entertainment business to submit themselves to the cruel and unusual punishment they'd receive as the butt of all these jokes—and for this particular roast, Jeff came up with a master stroke of casting. Hugh Hefner was a roast master's wet dream, presenting an endless possibility of jokes about getting old, getting laid and getting to do whatever the fuck you want for an entire fucking lifetime. Plus, it was also a master stroke because Hef once had a stroke while masturbating.

(A note of clarification: Although Mr. Hefner does in fact masturbate and did in fact have a stroke, there is no conclusive proof that these two events took place at the same time.)

If you remember, this was an interesting period in the history of American comedy. Basically, it was a dark, nothing time, because all of the comedy clubs and concert halls were dark and there was nothing for us comics to do. We weren't even telling jokes to each other. Typically, whenever there's a tragedy of national significance, or a crisis, or a health epidemic, there are dozens of jokes that immediately spring up and get passed around on the Internet, or over watercoolers, or on college campuses. A joke can go from lightbulb-over-the-head to viral, in no time. Readers might recall the terrible crash of the space shuttle, which coincided with the terrible rash of product-tampering deaths traced to tainted bottles of Tylenol, which led to the memorable punch line: "Gee, this is a terrible year for capsules."

Or, when Rock Hudson died, and the joke everyone was telling was, "Rock Hudson had no friends, but he had Nabors up the ass."

(Note to publisher: the misspelling of *neighbors* is intentional. It refers to the legendary Jim Nabors, TV's *Gomer Pyle*. In fairness to Mr. Nabors I have no reason to believe he is actually gay. In fact, I offered to suck his dick once and he turned me down. I don't know whether this was because he is straight or because he looked at me and realized I was Gilbert Gottfried.)

As long as I'm doing Rock Hudson jokes, I'll slip in another—the one about the doctor who had just prescribed that he drink a gallon of prune juice each day.

"Will that help my AIDS, doctor?" Rock Hudson asks.

"No," the doctor replies, "but it'll remind you what your asshole is for."

But this was different. There were no viral jokes because the world was still in shock. Everyone was numb, even comedians. It was a sad, uneasy period in our nation's history, especially in New York City, which had been the site of the most devastating of these attacks. We celebrities and semi-celebrities didn't know what to do with ourselves. There was even talk of canceling the Emmy Awards that year, until someone realized there was still a buck to be made, whether or not we were in a time of national mourning. Besides, if you didn't hand out Emmy Awards to hardly deserving television personalities, the terrorists would have won—and as far as I knew, Osama bin Laden didn't have a suitable mantel for an Emmy Award. Also, I don't think he was nominated that year.

There was a lot of tension and uncertainty in the Grand Ballroom of the New York Hilton when the roast finally got under way, but I believe most of this had to do with the presence of Ice-T as one of the presenters. He can be a menacing fellow. I can't be sure, but I believe Jeff Ross, Freddie Roman and the Friars Club roast committee invited him because he was a bad-ass black guy with lots and lots of bling, and his appearance at the roast might distract us from the Arab comics who were on the bill with us that evening.

I was scheduled to go last in the program, which was just as well with me. Usually, I like to get my performance out of the way, so I can turn my attention to playing with myself or rubbing up against some of the beautiful young starlets who tend to show up at these things, but here I really felt for the comics who had to go on first. People seemed unable or unwilling to laugh. It's like they were waiting to give each other permission. Of course, I suppose it's possible that the people they'd gotten to kick off the roast weren't very funny, but I remember thinking there were a few good lines being tossed around up there on the podium, and no one was responding to them.

The Friars Club always puts together an interesting guest list for its annual celebrity roast, and this year's event was no exception. There were the usual character-actor-types like Danny Aiello, Keith David, and Vincent Pastore and Joe Pantoliano from *The Sopranos*. There were the usual fringe show-business-types like Donald Trump, Dr. Joyce Brothers, the Amazing Kreskin, the artist LeRoy Neiman, MTV's Carson Daly, Patty Hearst (another famous heir of William Randolph Hearst), and Kiss guitarist Ace Frehley.

Like I said, an odd mix.

Jimmy Kimmel was the master of ceremonies. In his opening remarks, he said, "What can you say about Hef that hasn't already been mumbled incoherently by thousands of young women with his cock in their mouths?"

On any other night, people would have been doing spit-takes and choking on their food, because Hugh Hefner was such an easy, obvious target, but this was a tough assignment. There was laughter, but it was mostly polite laughter. Embarrassed laughter. Sheepish laughter. Basically, a whole bunch of different kinds of laughters—none of which, I'm afraid, are among the best kinds of laughters.

My favorite line in the early going was delivered by Alan King, one of the great Friars Club old-timers, who said that Hugh Hefner had smelt more beaver than a furrier—a killer line that was only warmly received, which made me feel bad because I always liked Alan King. He came up to me later that night and put his arm around me and told me my own personal joke. He took out his trademark cigar and said, "A Pakistani dies and goes to heaven. He's standing at the Pearly Gates, talking to Saint Peter. He says, 'I wish to speak to Jesus Christ.' And Saint Peter turns his head and yells, 'Jesus, your cab is here!'"

When it was finally my turn, I decided to fuck with Ice-T, because it's not often that a small, whiny Jew gets to fuck with a menacing black man without fearing for his life. I pointed to where he was sitting on the dais and said, "Ice-T did my whole act, but I'll do it anyway. I'm gonna follow you white motherfuckers home and rape you fucking white bitches."

Then, I waited for the people to stop their nervous laughing and said, "See, it's such a strong bit, it still works."

I worked my way around the room, saying unpleasant things about the various people in attendance. At some point, I landed on Hef, the guest of honor, so I said some things about him. I said, "Hugh Hefner doesn't need Viagra. He needs cement. He needs to take an ice cream stick and tape it to his dick and use it as a splint."

I said, "Hugh Hefner is so old his first condom was made out of bark."

I told some dirty jokes. I told some not-so-dirty jokes. I told some funny jokes. And I told some not-so-funny jokes, judging by the reaction of the crowd. It was hit-and-miss, but for the most part things seemed to be going well—or, at least, as well as they could have gone under the circumstances, because everyone was still in shock. But then I decided that doing well wasn't really enough, so I dug a little deeper. I said, "Tonight, I'll be using my Muslim name, Hasn't Been Laid. Which reminds me, I have to leave early tonight, because I'm going to Los Angeles. I couldn't get a direct flight. We have to make a stop at the Empire State Building first."

It was the joke that stopped time. Really.

For a long, terrible moment, there was a long, terrible silence. I had no idea what to expect, coming out with a line like that, but I expected . . . something. Instead, for the moment . . . nothing. This one little line had completely changed the mood of the room. From where I stood at the podium, I could actually feel people jumping back in their seats. I could feel chairs moving, rustling. There was a giant gasp, like a huge sucking sound, taking all the air out of the room. There was grumbling, and lots of nervousness. There was hissing. From the back of the ballroom, one person yelled, "Too soon!"

Then people started booing, and hissing some more . . . echoing the same sentiment. All of a sudden, I was the most wanted man in America—only here what these people most wanted me to do was leave.

You have to realize, I'd never really *had* the crowd. I was just mildly amusing them. Probably they were all being polite and waiting for me to finish so we could all go home. But now they'd gone in the complete opposite direction. Now it looked like I was about to be set upon by an angry lynch mob—made up primarily of rich, white, old entertainers.

Now, when I first heard this one guy in the back shout out "Too soon!" I of course thought I hadn't taken a long enough pause between the setup and the punch line. I heard it as constructive criticism, and I could have kicked myself. I thought, *Damn, it should have been, ". . . we have to make a stop at the [two, three, four, five . . .] Empire State Building."* It felt to me like Lesson One, and I was ashamed of myself for not realizing it.

Clearly, I had now lost the audience entirely, and it felt to me there might be a riot, so without any logic, or perhaps under the misguided notion that it would be a good idea to make these people even angrier, I shrugged my shoulders and said, "Awww . . . what the fuck do you care?"

People told me later that at this point I started moving my arms like a lunatic, or like I was conducting an orchestra, but I have no recollection of this. I watched the tape afterward and it seemed to me there might have been a swarm of gnats flying around the podium at just that moment, and I was frantically trying to shoo them away.

Then, for no good reason, I launched into a retelling of a famous joke that was known to be one of the most offensive, outrageous, off-putting jokes in the history of comedy. In my defense, all these years later, I can only say that it seemed like a good idea at the time.

People also told me later that there was an unusually long point of pause, between the booing and what happened next—that is, if you don't count all of that arm flailing. That happened right away. But I didn't say anything for the longest while. It was so long that people had time to think that maybe the microphone wasn't working—or, more likely, that someone had thought to shut it off before I could say anything else.

But I finally opened my mouth and went on with the show.

"Okay," I said, after my too long pause and the people had seemed to settle down a little bit. "A talent agent is sitting in his office. A family walks in. A man, woman, two kids, and their little dog. And the talent agent goes, 'What kind of act do you do?'"

Without any introduction or fanfare or warning, I'd launched into a bit that would either send my career off a steep comedy cliff, after which I would never be heard from again, or leave me to be ripped apart by the mob of angry old fucks who hadn't quite managed to leave the Grand Ballroom in a huff just yet. The bit was a timeless vaudevillian joke that was well known in comedy circles. For as long as I could remember, it was referred to with great reverence simply by its punch line: "The Aristocrats." Once in a while, you'd hear it told as "The Sophisticados," and on Wikipedia it suggests that it sometimes goes by the kicker "The Debonairs," but most people know it as "The Aristocrats." That is, people who tell jokes for a living know it this way. People who don't tell jokes for a living don't really know about it at all—or at least they didn't, until Penn Jillette and Paul Provenza made a documentary about it, featuring all these different comedians, telling all these different versions of the joke, and putting their own little spins and flourishes on it. The movie made it seem like the joke was a beloved jazz piece, and that every comic brought his own style to it, which I guess was true enough.

In the documentary, a bunch of comics remarked that the joke was like a secret handshake among comedians, and it talked about how we tried to one-up each other with our retellings backstage, between shows. It was only rarely told onstage, to general audiences, and was mostly passed back and forth among comics, looking to impress or shock or otherwise entertain their peers.

Here's an interesting side note: some years earlier, I told the joke to Richard Belzer's brother, Len, who kept asking me to tell it again. And again. Len just loved the crap out of that joke, and every time we got together he asked me to tell it. Each time out, I told it a little differently, depending on what was going on in my head at the time, or in the world, or in the room where I was doing the telling. One day Len came up to me and said, "Gilbert, this joke is just so hysterical, and it never comes out the same way twice. It gets more disgusting, more hilarious every time I hear it."

I said, "Gee, thank you, Len. I knew there was a reason I

liked hanging out with you. Now, if you don't mind, say some more nice things about me."

He said, "No, really. I'm serious. You know what you should do? You should make a film of you just telling this one joke, over and over."

And I thought, *Yeah, there's a great idea for a movie.*

Once again, what the hell did I know?

However, on this night in September 2001, most of the audience at the New York Hilton had never heard the joke. Not only that—they hadn't heard *of* the joke. I hadn't planned on telling it, but I'd dug such an impossible hole for myself with my Empire State Building joke that it was the only thing I could think of to pull myself out. It was like a crutch, that joke, and I guess I thought I could just beat people over the head with it. I didn't even think about it on any kind of conscious level. I just went for it. The other comics must have known where I was going with this, but everyone else was in for a big surprise.

For those readers who've still never heard the joke, I'm afraid I can't do it justice on the page. Why? Well, the joke itself is nothing much. Really, it's mostly a nonjoke. That's one of the reasons it's become such a staple, and a favorite of comedians, because it's the ultimate antijoke. It's all in the setup, in the telling. The idea is, if you can tell this joke well, you can tell any joke well. If you can amuse your friends, jaded comedy professionals, then you can amuse just about anybody.

The premise of the joke is basic: an apparently clean-cut family visits a talent agent, hoping to break into show business. The talent agent asks about the nature of the family's act, so the family proceeds to demonstrate. This takes us to the jazz part of the joke, only in most versions it's more like porn, because the family members usually just rip off their clothes and start sucking and fucking each other in every unimaginable way. Even the dog gets in on the fun. The idea is to be as disgusting and degenerate as possible, with everyone in the family going at each other and exchanging bodily fluids like they're at a Mamas & the Papas reunion. Bowel movements, urine, semen, snot, spittle, sweat . . . there are buckets and buckets of the stuff, all coming and going, in and out of every orifice, until finally the family is whipped and spent and collapses in exhaustion on the other side of the talent agent's desk.

At the ultimate climax, the talent agent very reasonably says, "Well, that's an interesting act. What do you call yourselves?"

At this, the father, the mother, the son, the daughter and the dog all lift themselves proudly from the pile of shit, piss, semen and sweat where they're lying and take a great big bow and say, "The Aristocrats!"

Well, the whole time I was telling this joke, in my own skillful way, the mood of the room started to change all over again. The people who had been recoiling in their seats, horrified at my Empire State Building joke, were now laughing their heads off. Rob Schneider fell off his chair he was laughing so hard, which really wasn't such a big deal because he's one of the few comics shorter than me and he didn't have very far to fall.

By the time I was finished the place was pretty much exploding with laughter.

A week later, a critic for *The New York Observer* gave me

one of the best reviews of my career, writing that I had turned the joke into "an extended bacchanal of bodily fluids, excrement, bestiality and sexual deviance." I had no idea what most of those words meant, but they sounded pretty good, strung together like that.

After that, the critic had some more nice things to say. "Mr. Gottfried plumbed the darkest crevices he could find," he wrote—which I think he meant in a good way, even though you might think that plumbing all those dark crevices might be seen as a negative. "He riffed and riffed until people in the audience were coughing and sputtering and sucking in great big gulps of air. Tears ran through the Hilton ballroom, as if Mr. Gottfried had performed a collective tracheotomy on the audience, delivering oxygen and laughter past the grief and ash that had blocked their passageways. . . . Then he brought it home."

I could go on and on, but at some point the *New York Observer* guy stopped writing.

People who were there have called my rendition of the joke "breathtaking"—and who am I to argue with them? Certainly, people were gasping for air, so I guess it's an accurate description. It was as if everything that had happened earlier in the evening—the fits and starts of the other comics, my own offensive jokes—had set the audience up for my rousing performance, and I killed. I know, I know . . . it sounds like I'm bragging, but this is my fucking book, so it's allowed.

(Feel free to join in and pile on the praise.)

People who weren't there and who tried to attach big words to explain the impact of my performance have called it "cathartic"—and once again, I can't argue. At first, I wasn't even sure what that word meant. I knew there was a word that would get close to describing the emotional release we all felt in that ballroom that evening, but I was going for "catatonic." I don't think I was in school the day we learned "cathartic."

Now, looking back, it's hard to say which came first, the documentary or my rousing performance at the Hugh Hefner roast, which readers might remember was featured as the centerpiece of the movie. (When the movie came out, one reviewer suggested that if an Academy Award could be handed out for telling a dirty joke, it should go to me.) It's a classic chicken-or-egg question. The movie was already in development, of course, and this Hugh Hefner roast came early on in the process, but I prefer to think I was the complete inspiration. Once again, it's my fucking book. I'll say what I want.

And speaking of saying what I want, did I mention that I was good friends with President Hoover? (Note to publisher, with a name like Hoover, perhaps we should consider a blow job joke here. Or have we exceeded our quota?)

I wasn't convinced that there was a movie in all of this, but Penn was persistent, so I signed on. He even convinced me to participate for free—making the movie itself one of Penn Jillette's greatest magic tricks. It still kills me, that trick, because once *The Aristocrats* movie became a surprise hit, I kept reminding myself that I wasn't making a dime from it. Like every family member in every version of the Aristocrats joke, I definitely got fucked in the ass.

Clip'n' Save Joke no. 17 ✂----------------

A little boy walks into his parents' bedroom while they are having sex. The little boy gasps, but the father continues humping away, laughing.

The next day, the father passes the little boy's room and sees that the little boy is fucking his ninety-year-old grandmother. The father gasps, so the son turns and says, "Not so funny when it's *your* mother, huh?"

ENCORE

Another Slice of Pizza and a Grape Drink

So there you have it. My book. Not bad, huh? Especially for my first book. It would even be impressive for my second or third book, I think. By the fourth or fifth book, though, I'll probably do a better job. By then I'll *really* have the hang of this book writing business. By then this one will pale by comparison.

Like I said at the beginning, I had modest goals for my first literary effort. Once again, at the very least I wanted it to be like a slice of pizza and a grape drink, and as many people know I've made a career out of reaching for the very least. The grape drink has nothing in it that can be considered of nutritional value. Same here. And a slice of pizza is like a blow job. Even a bad one is still pretty good. The only difference between a slice of pizza and a blow job is I can remember the last time I had a slice of pizza.

We've covered a lot of ground in these pages, in case you haven't been paying attention. We've laughed. We've cried. We've come to terms. Hopefully, we've all learned a little something about ourselves and what it means to be alive. Also hopefully, we've celebrated the simple beauties of self-love and self-absorption, which I'm happy to report often go hand in hand. Along the way, I've shared some of my thoughts and experiences. I've invited you, dear reader, into my head and heart. A few of you have even received an invitation into my pants. You know who you are. I've yet to hear back from you on this, but you shouldn't have too much trouble finding me. I'm the guy who wrote this book, remember? My picture's on the cover. Make a few calls and figure it out.

If you have an opportunity to tell your friends and relations about the book we've just enjoyed together, I encourage you to do so. There's a lot riding on this, and not just for me personally. It's not about the money. Well, okay . . . maybe it *is* about the money, but only a little, and the reason it's only a little about the money is because the publisher is paying me only a little.

If you must know, I'm doing this book mostly as a public service. Anyway, that's what I've been telling myself, to justify the time and effort. The way it's supposed to work is that every time someone buys a copy, an angel gets its wings. Also, for every tree the publisher knocks down and turns into paper to produce one of my books, we plant another one . . . in Israel! I made it a matter of contract, when we were negotiating my book deal. That's how strongly I feel about my Jewish heritage. Of course, if I was making a little more money on this deal, I'd plant some trees for Arab terrorists. This way, the Arabs could enjoy some shade while waiting for their prophet. Jews don't have to wait. We already know how to make a profit.

Oh, which reminds me. I have a joke. (Right now, I can hear all of you readers saying, "Finally!")

All kidding aside (which will probably be my *final* kidding aside, since I'm running out of pages), there's always room for one more joke, and here it is:

Two Arab terrorists are sitting together, sharing pictures of their kids. One says, "This is my five-year-old daughter." The other one says, "This is my three-year-old son." Then both terrorists sigh, and shake their heads and say, "They blow up so fast, don't they?"

Please realize, I don't mean to come across as anti-Arab with this one last joke. I'll have you know, I've seen every episode of *Make Room for Daddy*.

Let me get back to the public service part of this book deal. My idea was to sell tons and tons of books, destroying acres and acres of inconsequential American forest, and at the other end of the transaction we'd plant a bunch of trees in the homeland of my people. After that, the trees would grow and flourish, and in a couple years, after I'd done some growing and flourishing of my own, I could travel to Israel before I die and take a nice walk in the park where my trees had been planted and enjoy a short nap in the shade of my own making. Who knows, I might even be inspired to sit beneath one of my trees and read a book. By some other comic. Who's not as funny as me.

It's the circle of life.

And the best part is it's environmentally correct. It's just made out of paper, this book, so you can recycle it. You can even recycle some of the jokes—because God knows that's what I've been doing, all these years. This gives me great satisfaction, because being green is so fashionable these days. A lot of the hotter, better-looking young actresses in Hollywood seem to be in favor of it, so I'm all for it. Anything to improve my chances. Now that I think about it, it doesn't even matter to me if you've read the whole thing, from beginning to end. I don't care, as long as you bought it. That could be the entire extent of your commitment, as far as I'm concerned. If you took it out of the library and then didn't read it, then we'd have a problem. But as long as you've paid your way, do whatever you want. Rip the pages from the spine and use them to wipe your ass, for all I care—although, now that I think about *this* it feels to me like something I should have known, going in. It would have been helpful. I mean, if you weren't going to read the book anyway, I wouldn't have gone to all that trouble to put so many words on each and every page. I could have left all the pages blank.

(Note to critics: that "left all the pages blank" line is my gift to you. You're welcome.)

Extra-Special Bonus ✂ Clip 'n' Save Joke to Justify the Title

Okay, dear reader. You've been a terribly good sport about this. You've kept turning the page, and turning the page, asking only to be somewhat entertained. I believe I've held up my end. I hope you agree, but even if you don't I must admit you've been very patient. You've come all this way, not knowing what the hell I meant by slapping such a nonsense title on the cover of this book.

Well, I've been wondering the same thing, so to explain myself I'll treat all of us to one last joke. It's one of those repeat-after-me jokes that are popular on school playgrounds. For this one, which is best appreciated by first- or second-graders, or readers with a first- or second-grade mentality, you're supposed to repeat the phrase "Rubber Balls and Liquor" after every line. Then, at the end, you're supposed to laugh uproariously, which of course is what you're supposed to do at the end of all my jokes—but you don't need me to tell you that. Got it? Here goes . . .

What did you have for breakfast?
"Rubber balls and liquor."
What did you have for lunch?
"Rubber balls and liquor."
What did you have for dinner?
"Rubber balls and liquor."
What are you going to do to your girlfriend tonight?
"Rubber balls and liquor."

Extra-Special Bonus ✂------- Clip 'n' Save Joke to Justify the Title

Get it? Hmmm . . . maybe you didn't tell it right. Or maybe you're too old. Try telling it to a six-year-old and see what kind of reaction you get. If you don't have one of your one, borrow a niece or a nephew or a kid from the neighborhood. If you still don't get a laugh, try that E.T. joke I shared earlier, about how Reese's Pieces taste like cum on his planet. Or the one where the guy fucks his dying wife up the ass. If he doesn't laugh at one of those, it's possible there's something wrong with the kid. I'm just saying.

Now that I think about it, something has always troubled me about this joke. Even when I was on the school playground, preparing for my career as a professional comedian, it troubled me. Why? Well, it's the only joke in the history of comedy that refers to a pair of breasts as "balls." This makes no sense. Never in my life have I seen an attractive girl with nice tits walk down the street and heard a bunch of construction-worker-types say, "Gee, get a load of the balls on that one." It's the kind of comment that could be misunderstood in polite society, which is why when I see an attractive girl with nice tits walk down the street I always say, "Gee, get a load of the testicles on that one!"

But that's just me.

CLOSING CREDITS

"I'd Like to Thank the Academy"

This is the "thanks" part of the book. It's like one of those long acceptance speeches at the Oscars. In fact, if this part gets long and boring and you're lucky enough to be near a piano, please feel free to tinkle a few notes on the keyboard to let me know it's time to wrap up and get off the stage.

You see, giving thanks is like leaving tips or giving gifts on Christmas. You really don't want to, but it's expected of you and you're too much of a pussy not to.

So here goes. Most importantly, I'd like to thank my Lord and Savior Jesus Christ. In the middle of this book, when I thought there were no more places I could fit the words "cock" or "cunt," He came down and pointed to several spots I had apparently missed. Turns out He has a really good eye for that sort of thing.

On a more earthly plane, I'd like to thank my parents, because without them I would never have been born. (A final note to readers: I'll now give everyone a few seconds to say, "And why would that have been bad?") I'd also like to thank my sisters, Arlene and Karen. They didn't help with the book, but they like seeing their names in print. So there.

I'd like to thank Marc Guss and Dan Strone, as well as Marc Resnick and everyone at St. Martin's Press for waiting until I left the room to say, "Who thought a Gilbert Gottfried book was a good idea?"

I'd like to thank a man who stood behind me . . . in the men's room, when I was trying to pee.

I'd like to thank Dan Paisner, for stopping me every three words to say, "Can you talk a little slower?"

They say that behind every truly great man there's an overbearing Jew bitch who screeches, "Gilbert, shut off the television and get back to work on the book! We've had the same dining room set for an hour and a half! It's time to get a newer, much more expensive set!" So, thank you to my wife, Dara.

Lastly, I'd like to thank my nephew Graham, for yelling "Ca Ca Booty!" at his preschool teacher. A few more outbursts like that and St. Martin's Press will offer him a book deal.